JOHN NASH

John Nash painting in his
studio at Bottengoms in 1975.
Photo: Anthea Sieveking

JOHN NASH

Sir John Rothenstein

Macdonald & Co
London & Sydney

Text © Sir John Rothenstein 1983

First published in Great Britain in 1983 by
Macdonald & Co (Publishers) Ltd
London & Sydney

Maxwell House
74 Worship Street, London EC2A 2EN

ISBN 0 356 09780 3

Produced by Bettina Tayleur Ltd
1 Newburgh Street, London W1V 1LH
Text set in Garamond by Input Typesetting Ltd, London SW19
Picture reproduction by Bright Arts HK Ltd, Hong Kong
for Imago Publishing Ltd, 103 High Street, Thame, Oxfordshire
Printed and Bound by South China Printing Co, Hong Kong

Editor: Anthony Eyre
Picture research: Sara Rodgers
Design: Tom Carter

Contents

TO
ELIZABETH AND LUCY

Acknowledgements

My warmest thanks and appreciation are due to the following individuals and organisations for their generous help and co-operation in gathering together the material for this book. In particular, I would like to offer my heartfelt thanks to Anthony Eyre, the editor of the book.

John Nash's literary executors, John Lewis (who besides giving me valuable information, lent me a large quantity of his correspondence), David Pearce and Colin Benham; David Wolfers, John Nash's art executor, for permission to reproduce the illustrations; George Wingfield Digby for permission to publish letters of Paul Nash; Ronald Blythe for much valuable information; Noel Carrington for permission to publish letters from his sister Dora Carrington to John Nash and for valuable information about their relationship; the Trustees of the Imperial War Museum for permission to quote from documents and sound records in their possession, and to Mrs Vivienne Crawford, formerly of the Museum's Department of Art, for enabling me to see pictures by John Nash not on exhibition and for the loan of material relevant to his work as an Official War Artist in both World Wars.

I am indebted also to Jennifer Andrews, Edward Bawden, Natalie Bevan, Mrs E. Blond, Blond Fine Art, Robert Buhler, Sir Andrew Carnwath, Lady Cranbrook, Mrs Luise Curtis, Anthony d'Offay, Barbara Langston, The Minories (Victor Batte-Lay Trust), Anstice Shaw, Anthea Sieveking, Janet Stone, and Vincent Turner.

Sir John Rothenstein
July 1983

CHAPTER I
Iver Heath

A book devoted to accounts of how painters and draughtsmen began their careers would make entertaining and, in certain cases, surprising reading. It is often assumed that when boys and girls show talent at school they are given opportunities to develop it, before they proceed to art college, after which, with a greater or lesser degree of success, they are launched upon the world.

Of John Nash it would hardly be an overstatement to say that, although from his early years highly visual, he became an artist through favourable circumstances rather than boyhood determination. Had things been otherwise he might well have followed some different calling.

John Northcote Nash was born on 11 April 1893, the younger of the two sons of William Harry Nash and his wife Caroline Maude, daughter of Captain Milbourne Jackson, of the Royal Navy. John's elder brother Paul was born on 11 May 1889, and his sister Barbara Milbourne in 1895. Their father, born in 1841 of a long established Buckinghamshire family, was called to the Bar in 1873, becoming Revising Barrister for Gloucestershire and later Recorder of Abingdon. All three children were born in a house then called Ghuznee Lodge, in Sunningdale Gardens, Earl's Court, West London, where the family lived until 1901. In *Outline: An Autobiography and Other Writings* Paul described Ghuznee Lodge as 'a pariah of a house, with its outlandish name and pretentious conservatory where nothing, ever, would grow'. His description of it, from which this is only a brief extract, conveys not only dislike of the house, but also intimates, however indirectly, a dislike of towns which the brothers shared. Their happiest hours were spent in Kensington Gardens, which they visited daily with their nurse, Harriet Luckett.

The family left Ghuznee Lodge for Iver Heath, Buckinghamshire, moving into Wood Lane House, which Harry Nash had built in the hope that his increasingly ill wife

The Nash children: Paul
(standing), John and their
sister Barbara, photographed
c.1900 with their nurse,
Harriet Luckett.
Collection Ronald Blythe

would benefit from a rural environment. Not only was
her condition grievous but it was so financially exacting,
especially for a man whose legal practice was dwindling,
that when she was sent to a nursing home the house had to
be let. Harry and Paul lived in lodgings nearby, John returning during the school holidays. Caroline Nash died on 4
February 1910.

John Nash attended Langley Place, a preparatory school
between Slough and Uxbridge, from 1905 until 1909, as a
boarder towards the end of the period, before going to
Wellington College where he remained for two years. 'Why
I was sent to a military school,' he said to a friend, 'my
father never told me.' But he believed that it was due to the
financial help of an uncle who made it a condition.

Wellington, however, made a contribution to his eventual
decision to become an artist. 'I went in for the Botany Prize
[which he won] in order to avoid cricket. Some sport had
to be played and I chose fives. With freedom to ramble and
collect specimens I spent two agreeable Summer Terms.'[1]

He was also as he put it, 'saturated' by the Pre-Raphaelites, doubtless owing to Paul's enthusiasm for them,
reflected in designs for book-plates, made between 1907 and
1910, in which the influence of Rossetti is conspicuous.

John's own enthusiasm was expressed in an essay on Pre-Raphaelitism, the quality of which was recognised by a Wellington master, a Mr Tallboys. He occasionally invited John to visit him at his home on Sundays, when they would discuss art and literature, and he used also to show him reproductions of the Old Masters.

The Nash family's connections with the arts were few; one was through John's aunt, the Hon. Augusta Bethell, daughter of the first Lord Westbury. Edward Lear had been deeply in love with her, but considered himself too old and ugly to propose; however he gave her a large and varied collection of his works. She married Thomas Arthur Nash, her father's biographer. Lear had been a friend of the family, so when Paul and John used to visit the house of their 'Aunt Gussie', as she was known, they were fascinated by his comic drawings and the sketches illustrating his Nonsense Verses which she used to read to them. They treasured the copies which she gave them of Lear's books.

During his school holidays John used to frequent, among other museums, the Victoria and Albert, where he was particularly impressed by the watercolours of Cotman and De Wint. He early began to make drawings, both landscape and comic. Paul was so impressed by the latter that in 1910, during John's first year at Wellington, he took several to show to my father, William Rothenstein, whose response was encouraging. The comic drawings with which he used to illustrate his letters delighted his family. At that time, however, there was no thought of his becoming an artist. During his last year at Wellington, Paul thus described his brother:

> . . . he seemed suddenly to have matured. No one knew what he would do. The wildest schemes had been suggested for his future, the Church, a diplomatic career, journalism, but at present we were content to say he would probably go to Oxford. He showed already one quality, the mentality of a scholar, but as yet it was no more than an attitude.[2]

He was, wrote his brother, 'delicate and had auburn hair'; his cousins 'admired his dark fine profile, while his scholarly, slightly elaborate manner of talking intrigued them'.[3]

Their father, already in financial difficulties, could in any case hardly be expected to maintain two artists. After John had failed to secure a place at an Oxford college the possibility of entering a solicitor's office was discussed, but his father decided that his means were insufficient to meet the cost. In any case, more attracted by writing than the law, John preferred to become a journalist, and in the summer

of 1912 served for a few months as an unpaid apprentice on the *Middlesex & Buckinghamshire Advertiser*, in which one of his drawings was reproduced. He left in August, without occupation or prospects.

Although he never became a professional writer, his occasional published writings show his competence, while his letters – he maintained a very extensive correspondence with his wife and friends – showed a command of prose, casual in style, highly evocative and ranging from occasional quotations from the Greek to obviously deliberate mistakes made for effect.

Besides writing he became intensely interested in music, 'he at once began to read the lives of the great musicians,' wrote Paul 'and later, by some seemingly miraculous and certainly painful method he learned to play the piano and experimented with wind instruments'.[4] This interest proved lifelong.

His position on the local paper had never been thought of as other than temporary and Paul became steadily more convinced that he should be an artist. With this end in view they called, while John was still with the *Advertiser*, on Grant Richards, the publisher, taking with them a number of John's drawings and writings. Richards dismissed the writings and praised the drawings, much to the elder boy's pleasure. Paul's attitude is clearly apparent in a piece of his unpublished writing, evidently of a considerably later date:

About this time John began to make what was known in the family as 'comic drawings'. They were quite casual at first, drawn on odd pieces of paper usually from father's revision books in pen and ink and consisted of various

An Accident c.1912
Chalk and wash, 6½″ x 12″, signed. This early drawing is typical of Nash's charming naive style at this period; it also illustrates his sense of the comic and his interest in the countryside and in agriculture, two things which were to remain with him throughout his life.
Bevan Collection/Photo: Royal Academy of Arts

Lloyd George in Hell
Watercolour, 15¾″ x 10¾″,
c.1913. This probably dates
from the period when Nash
was working on the *Middlesex
and Buckinghamshire
Advertiser.*
Photo: Anthony d'Offay

sorts of ludicrous happenings, not unlike James Thurber
has invented at a much later period and in another
country. Gradually these drawings took on a more
purposeful look. Watching them closely as I did I became
aware of something more than an original 'comic' vision
which Jack undoubtedly possessed. They began to show
an intrinsic sense of plan and decoration. More than this
the incidental features of the comic events, specially forms
of natural objects in landscape for instance, even some
animals seemed to be drawn with an intuitive understanding which made them extraordinarily convincing. I
noticed these developments with growing interest. Then
one day, I came upon a small sketch made on Jack's
excursion as a reporter, a little view of flooded meadows
under a night sky with a hedge of trees mounting in the
foreground. The moment I saw it I was convinced my
brother was an artist and must be given every chance to
work out whatever talent was in him. I remember the

excitement of this discovery and feeling so confident I could not be mistaken that I told my father there need be no more speculation as to Jack's career, he was going to be an artist, in time . . . from that time, Jack continued to grow as an artist with suprising speed.[5]

Describing to me, at some point in the middle nineteen-fifties, his response to Paul's determination that he should become an artist, John said, 'I must have a very malleable character, for I'd never thought seriously of becoming an artist, but I at once agreed, and set about making a landscape in watercolour as well as more comic drawings. Paul wasn't happy at the Slade and he opposed my going there or to any art school, and he used to tell me how lucky I was to begin free from the disadvantages of conventional training. All the same', he added, 'I wish I'd had the advantage of training of some kind'.

Paul had also sent a packet of John's drawings to his friend Gordon Bottomley, who in his reply, dated 7 July 1912, praised them highly, saying: 'He has not only a good sense of decorative composition of his masses, but his blacks have a beautiful quality and his pen-touch is crisp and clear and delicate and exquisitely balanced. . . . In facility and lucidity and directness of expression, and in his faculty for keeping his material untroubled, he has the advantage over you, but of course it remains to be seen if he can preserve these qualities when he has as much to say as you have'.[6]

This letter shows rare perception: not many who saw the work of this mere beginner would have recognised the qualities inherent in it. Paul replied, a week or so later:

Jack is very 'set up for the rest of 'is natural' as the vulgar have it, upon your high praise – I don't mean he has swollen his headpiece, for he ever expresses a mild suprise at any appreciation of his drawings, which he does at odd times on odd bits of paper when he has nothing else to do. I, from time to time, raid his desk or the corners of the room and collect the odd bits of paper rather like a park-keeper in Kensington Gardens, and after a sorting of chaff from grain tho' to be sure it's all 'chaff' I select the best & cut them into a decent shape & mount them. At first Jack used to be so delighted at the good appearance of his drawings when mounted that he fully believed it was entirely owing to the way I set them up & drew lines round them; gradually it dawned on him tho' that it must be he had done a good drawing – this is a pity because he now becomes a little too conscious & careful, with the result his designs are not so naive and simple.

Encounter at Uxbridge Station
Pen and watercolour, 15″ x
11″, signed. Dating from about
1913, this painting shows how
comic figure drawing and
landscape combined in Nash's
early work.
*Private Collection/Photo:
Anthony d'Offay*

At present he is working on the staff of a country
newspaper & gaining experience for a journalistic career.
All his abilities lie in that direction and he will tell you
his ambition is to be 'a man of letters'. He is very observant and writes excellent descriptions of things that strike
him, always with the same quaint touch you see in these
designs. He has so far done very little actual writing save
a few articles in the paper and some essays when he was
at Wellington. The work for the paper takes all his time &
he is riding about & reporting all over the country and
at all times of the day & night. Unfortunately his time is
up in August for this has been experience & work quite
unpaid as regards salary, and then I really don't know
what happens – a London paper I suppose is the next
thing – he likes regular work & routine, unlike me, &
works well; at the same time he is not constitutionally
robust & v. hard work in London would not be good
for him I fear. I myself have no doubt he has a most

interesting self to develop, & work to produce, but how & in what direction I really am not certain.[7]

This letter, in spite of the generosity it expresses towards his brother's potentialities as an artist, is also marked by a singular element of reserve, apparent in the last sentence. That element persisted over many years.

Late in 1937 I was commissioned to write a commentary to accompany a portfolio of reproductions by John Nash, similar to one that had appeared of Paul's work earlier that year. This project, which John warmly welcomed, resulted in a considerable correspondence in which Paul also took part. In a letter postmarked 31 January 1938, John comments on Paul's reaction to my article, particularly to my laudatory if somewhat commonplace introduction:

> I showed Paul your article as you permitted or suggested. . . . I must tell [you] that Paul did indeed question certain things in the article and seemed to think you had not 'got me right' as they say. He also thought that the length of the first part was a *drawback*, keeping the subject of the

The Allotment
Crayon, ink and watercolour, 15¼″ x 19″. Painted c.1914, this painting illustrates Nash's growing confidence in handling the abstract forms of landscape, in contrast with the continuing naivety of his figure style.
Private Collection/Photo: Anthony d'Offay

article waiting in the ante-room so to speak and that I was not a suitable person on which [sic] to hang a treatise of that nature. He read it very carefully and in detail and he is, as you know, very thorough on such matters. I find it difficult to write to you about this but I do assure you that the criticisms made were not done in any carping or ungrateful spirit. He said he would like to talk to you on the subject. He further declared that I was 'dumb' about myself, and very probably unhelpful and that he could tell you more about me in half an hour than any amount of interviews with me direct. I feel that it would be a tremendous help if you see him and I have warned him of your approach. . . . Personally I feel rather hopeless about the book altogether.

It is not my purpose to defend my introduction, though it is perhaps relevant to note that the subject was not 'kept waiting in the ante-room' but was 'on stage' from the first line. I told Paul how much I would value his opinion, and he and his wife invited my wife and me to lunch. He asked me to read the introduction aloud, which I did. He then said, with deliberation, 'It was I who encouraged Jack to be a painter; and I'm still not sure that I did rightly. I don't know whether he has a painter's imagination'. These words astonished me, and although he repeated his opinion several times in slightly different terms, I might have doubted having heard them correctly, had not my wife heard them also.

Shortly afterwards, he wrote me a long letter from his home in Eldon Road, Hampstead, dated 25 May, about various matters but referring yet again to 'the subject of your essay':

When J. left Wellington he was supposed to go to Oxford. The prospect fell through and no one seemed quite certain in what direction he would steer. By way of filling in time he took a job as reporter on a local newspaper and it was while he was at that peculiar game that he began to make frequent drawings. . . . I began to encourage him to do more of this sort of thing. All the same he went his own way mostly and I was careful not to try any special pressure. I think my own practice of continual drawing influenced him. We had drawn, as it were, side by side, since we could hold pencils. It was natural for him to fall in line again now that the interruptions of 'school' were over and we could spend more time together.

He then came across a Slade friend of mine, [Claughton] Pellew-Harvey[8]. They in turn became great

Threshing c.1914
Crayon, ink and watercolour,
11″ x 15¼″. An early example
of one of Nash's favourite
subjects.
Photo: Anthony d'Offay

friends and Pellew who had done much to help me in my first stages seemed able to get Jack going in earnest. They spent a holiday together – I think in Norfolk – and from this appeared the first authentic, convincing signs that Jack had something to say and was going to say it in the medium of some kind of art, as opposed to literature, or diplomacy or whatever other fields of operation had been considered for him. I remember I told my father when I had seen these first watercolours that he might as well make up his mind to it. Jack, I felt certain, was going to be an artist.

Pellew's example and encouragement continued and rapidly bore fruit.

J. adopted and enlarged for his purpose the techniques of watercolour washed over waxy chalk [crayon?] areas which he, Pellew, used so skillfully in his own work. But what he picked up from seeing me draw and paint and what he got from Pellew was the only schooling in art he ever had. From the beginning he was practically self-made.

What I miss in your account of J's development is any reference to the extraordinary vision of his first pictures.

They were, as any pictures ever were, the products of a true naivety; as authentic as the Douanier Rousseau's. If a number of these were collected they would represent a unique passage in the history of English art. . . .

I have no doubt that in this last letter Paul expressed his basic feelings towards his brother as an artist, his faith in his dedication and his powers of expression. Then why, it might be asked, devote so much space to so simple a matter? Because the issue is not quite so simple as it seems. If it were why should an ordinary little article have provoked expressions so contrary about its subject, and such an extensive correspondence? What survives of Paul's last letter is itself longer than the article.

The answer, I think, is that Paul's feelings towards John as an artist, however basically and continuously benevolent and admiring, also long remained complex and obsessional. Owing to the threat of war the portfolio of reproductions and its commentary was never published. However, I set down Paul's words without change in my essay on John in *Modern English Painters 2* (1956). John carefully checked this chapter; had he considered my quotation from our lunchtime conversation undesirable or irrelevant he would surely have recommended its omission.

Landscape with a Windmill Pencil and watercolour, 10¾″ x 15¼″. Dating from c.1914, this painting originates from one of Nash's expeditions to Norfolk with Claughton Pellew-Harvey; as such it should be compared to *Sheringham*, on page 34. *Anthony d'Offay*

Self-portrait, pen and ink, 8″ x
7½″, dated 1913 and signed
with a monogram.
Photo: Anthony d'Offay

CHAPTER II
Early Maturity

An extraordinary feature of the work of John Nash was the rapidity of its development. In July 1912 Paul was wondering whether his brother should become an artist or a writer, yet that very year one of his watercolours was accepted by the New English Art Club and sold. Also that year, he and Paul were invited to contribute to a book of reproductions entitled *Georgian Drawings*, a projected companion to *Georgian Poetry*, which was never published due to the outbreak of war. Both these books were edited by Edward Marsh, an influential patron in the art world, who became an important friend to John after they met early in 1914.

As a result of a chance encounter John carried out in 1912 a piece of work wholly dissimilar from anything he ever did before or since. Roger Fry was engaged on the restoration of 'The Picture Bearers', one of Mantegna's series of nine scenes from 'The Triumph of Caesar', at Hampton Court Palace, and Paul was assisting him. One day John came with him, and 'just as Paul was starting work, Fry came into the room, and saw John standing idly by and said . . . 'If your little brother would like to do a job of work today, he can get down on the floor & repaint the feet''.' 'So I got down', John Nash said, 'with tubes of Dr Colley's Mixture [and] started to work on the toes! I'm not very proud of that episode. Fancy him letting me loose on a painting like that!'[9].

In November, 1913, the brothers shared an exhibition, 'Drawings by Paul & John Nash', at the now long-defunct Dorien Leigh Gallery in Pelham Street, South Kensington (which they hired for eight days for £12-10-0). It was not a picture gallery but a shop run by two young men who sold lampshades, whom Paul had persuaded to house the exhibition. Paul had held, the previous year, an exhibition

DRAWINGS BY
PAUL & JOHN NASH

This poster (21½″ x 16½″) was painted by Paul and John Nash together in oils on canvas to advertise their joint exhibition at the Dorien Leigh Gallery in 1913. In the foreground are Paul (left) and John, and beyond are Rupert Lee with his future wife Rosalind, followed by Margaret Odeh (who later married Paul) and an unknown woman. The Wittenham Clumps beyond often appear in both brothers' work.
Private Collection

of drawings and watercolours, and begun to establish his reputation, but for John the Dorien Leigh exhibition represented the beginning of his career, although the admiration it evoked was directed towards both brothers.

'The brothers Nash are always interesting', wrote Walter Sickert pertinently, reviewing the London Group exhibition held two years later, 'Paul with his head, where a poet's should be, in the clouds, and John, like the child that a painter should be, putting his hand in his mouth to tell us what he has seen in the field or on the farm that afternoon'.

The exhibition at the Dorien Leigh Gallery was remarkably well attended by visitors likely to be of help in a variety of ways. It was warmly received by fellow artists, especially Harold Gilman, Charles Ginner, Spencer Gore and Robert Bevan, as well as Walter Sickert and my father, whom both brothers told me had encouraged a number of artists and collectors to attend; among the collectors, Sir Michael Sadler, one of the most perceptive, and Roger Fry, the most influential English art critic of the time. After its opening Paul wrote to Gordon Bottomley 'the show is already a success beyond our highest hopes. Twelve drawings sold or nearly half the exhibits! . . . Jack has now sold seven and I four, tho' in value my four make nearly as much as Jack's seven. . . . It is a great joy to us both we have so many expenses & there is so much to get – tempera paints, a stove for the studio . . . & now we are provided for'[10].

In not much over a year from becoming a full-time artist John had won a position of respect destined steadily to increase throughout his life. Such immediate recognition would have been unlikely without his close association with Paul, some four years his senior, who, unlike him, had received training at three art schools, including the Slade, where Stanley Spencer, Edward Wadsworth and a number of others destined to become notable figures were his actual or near contemporaries. Through Paul John met Ben Nicholson, besides the now greatly underestimated Eric Kennington and the all but forgotten Rupert Lee, who stimulated his addiction to music and improved his piano playing.

John used to visit the Slade, where the two brothers were often seen together, as Paul depicted them in a watercolour, wearing identical black suits, broad-brimmed black hats and carrying silver-handled canes. It was there that he formed one of the most intense friendships of his life, shared, although to a considerably lesser degree, by Paul. It was with Dora Carrington, a little of whose voluminous correspondence with John will be quoted later. In the same year,

'A rather smudgy drawing of my friend Barbara's two extraordinary brothers': Paul and John Nash visiting the Slade, drawn by Paul and signed with his monogram. Paul's rather Egyptian figure style reappears in the poster he and John painted to advertise their joint exhibition at the Dorien Leigh Gallery in 1913. *Photo: Anthony d'Offay*

Trees by the sea, Norfolk
Pencil and watercolour, 11″ x
10¼″. Painted around about
1914, this work is
representative of the paintings
Nash exhibited with the
Camden Town Group and the
London Group.
Photo: Anthony d'Offay

1913, he also formed a friendship with another Slade student, also of exceptional talent, Christine Kühlenthal, who some five years later was to become his wife.

These various circumstances, but primarily the success of the Dorien Leigh exhibition, brought him into the centre of the art world. In December 1913 he and Paul were invited to become members of the Friday Club, a former Chelsea studio, where painters, mainly members of the Bloomsbury Group, used to meet weekly to show one another their work and discuss it. The two brothers were also associated with the Camden Town Group, established in May 1911. When it was enlarged with the inclusion of Wyndham Lewis, the Vorticists and the Cubists to become the London Group, John was elected as a founder member, on 3 January 1914. Inevitably the amalgamation of such disparate bodies caused tensions. 'Fancy people joining', wrote Lucien Pissarro, who objected to Vorticists such as Wyndham Lewis and Wadsworth, 'with the idea of forming a teetotaller society and coming to the conclusion that in order not to be narrow-minded they must admit some drunkards'. John respected Wyndham Lewis for the precision of his draughtsmanship.

John had shown at the preliminary exhibition, held from 16 December 1913 until 19 January 1914 at the Brighton

Public Art Gallery, entitled 'The Camden Town Group & Others' – the 'Others' being the Wyndham Lewis-led Vorticists. About this exhibition Paul wrote to my father. 'And to crown all Spencer Gore [first President and a leading member of the Camden Town Group] has taken six of Jack's, six of mine. This is amusing – so we're English Post-Impressionists & Cubists are we?'

The first exhibition of the London Group opened on 5 March at the Goupil Gallery. It was a grand coalition of radicals: 'Gilman was the motive force', wrote C. R. W. Nevinson, a fellow member, 'slowly, but surely with the help of [T. E.] Hulme he gathered all the warring factions of Impressionists, Neo-Primitives, Vorticists, Cubists and Futurists. . . . I was elected secretary, Gore treasurer, and Gilman eventually accepted the presidency because Sickert, with his usual modesty, refused the honour'[11]. Gilman hoped that this exhibition would further his ambition to promote a degree of unity among serious Post-Impressionist artists who had hitherto belonged to small – and transitory groups, and bring together those called the 'Realists' such as the Camden Towners and the 'Formalists' such as the Vorticists. John Nash, who only began that year to work

Although self-taught, throughout his life John Nash's approach to painting was based on a professional technique derived from Gilman's advice at the outset of his career to work in the studio from drawings and studies. Here (left) a squared-up study dated 'Kimble 1922' and used for *The Moat, Grange Farm* (right, oil on canvas, 30″ x 20″).
Trustees of the Tate Gallery, London

seriously in oil paints, was a 'Realist' whose work Gilman particularly admired. He believed that he could help John to master the medium, which indeed he did, considering him, incidentally, an artist of greater promise than Paul.

In one respect, but that crucial, John observed Gilman's advice, almost invariably, for the rest of his life. This was not to paint directly from nature but from drawings, preferably watercolours, made on the spot; and the existence of scores of his studies of all periods, many of them very slight, carefully squared up, testify to the consistency with which he observed it. Gilman also gave the beginner further valuable technical advice, stressing, for instance, the importance of using paint unmixed with oil, and opaque rather than transparent colours. 'There's enough oil in the paint anyhow', he said.

John's association with Gilman, Ginner and Bevan, who together formed the Cumberland Market Group, remained close, although he was never fully in sympathy with Post-Impressionism. He exhibited with them in two rooms which

Gloucestershire Landscape
Oil on canvas, 19″ x 23½″, signed and dated 1914. This painting remained in Nash's possession throughout his life; in his will he left instructions that it should be given to a museum.
Ashmolean Museum, Oxford

they rented at 49 Cumberland Market, where Bevan made his well-known paintings of hay-carts; also at the Goupil Gallery in April 1915, which, for him, had one important result. Its proprietor, William Marchant, became his dealer and remained with him until he died, being succeeded by his wife until she, too, died in 1958.

Bevan was an extraordinarily benevolent friend. Many artists liked to exhibit in Paris, where he had shown at the *Salon des Independants*, and he was anxious that his friends should have an opportunity of doing likewise. Accordingly, in the spring of 1920 he and Ginner spent some weeks in Paris for the purpose of arranging an exhibition of the work of English painters. They were successful and *Peintres Modernes Anglais* was held in June and July 1921 at the Galerie E. Drouet. Besides Bevan, Ginner and Gilman (who had died in 1919), the work of several of their juniors, including John Nash, Edward Wadsworth and William Roberts, was represented.

The fact that John missed Fry's 'Manet & the Post-Impressionists', his first Post-Impressionist exhibition held at the Grafton Galleries from November 1910 until January 1911, and, in his own words, 'did not dream of visiting the second, which was held while I was constantly in London' (October 1912–January 1913), has sometimes invited the opinion that his work is marked by a provincial character. To speculate about the effects of experiences which never took place is generally unwise, but I am confident that the effect of whatever works of art he saw would have been minimal. The success of the Dorien Leigh exhibition enabled him, for instance, to pay a brief visit early in 1914 to Florence, where he frequented the Uffizi and was moved by many of the works of the great Italian masters; but even this visit proved of no significance as far as his own art was concerned.

There have long been many art historians and critics who, in spite of the work of Rembrandt, Blake, Turner, Constable, Courbet, Dégas and others, contend or assume that what primarily inspires a painter is the example of the work of his predecessors and contemporaries, rather than what he himself sees or imagines. There is indeed an element of truth in this contention, for there are innumerable artists whose work is predominantly derived from that of others. But there are many others scarcely so dependent – to take two modern examples, Francis Bacon and Edward Burra – whose incentive is their own highly individual way of seeing the world about them or their own imagination. But there are yet others objectively focussed on their subjects. Of

Trees in a Flood c.1915
Oil on canvas, 17½″ x 14¼″.
This was the first Nash
painting to enter a public
collection, when Sir Michael
Sadler donated it to the Leeds
City Art Gallery in 1915.
Leeds City Art Gallery

these John Nash was a notable example. In his earliest years
he was deeply preoccupied with the work of the brother to
whom he owed so much, interested in that of his friends,
but with painting in general he remained little concerned.

By 1915 he had had a number of successful exhibitions
and established himself as an artist. In that same year he
was first represented in a public collection when Sir Michael
Sadler gave one of his watercolours, 'Trees in a Flood', to
the City Art Gallery, Leeds. In the time since leaving school
indecision had given way to conviction, and John had developed a very personal style firmly based in the inspiration
of his subject matter rather than the influence of any outside
group or movement. Although with the passage of the years
the character of his painting underwent slight modification
this represented logical development rather than change.
Few artists, within a year or two of beginning to paint,
have evolved, as he did, a way of seeing, of representing
what he saw, which lasted until the end of a long and
productive working life with only slight modification of
style other than a tendency towards simplification of form.

CHAPTER III
Carrington

Until the end of his life John Nash was exceptionally responsive to the attractions of women. For many his emotions were transitory. There were two, however, for whom they were enduring and intense. The first was Dora Carrington. The second was his wife.

Carrington (she disliked her own christian name and would express her dislike of women being called by their christian names as an indication of inferiority, which did not inhibit her from calling men by theirs) was born in Hereford in 1893. At the age of seventeen, having shown an ardent preoccupation with drawing, she went to the Slade. There she proved herself an artist of rare talent, exemplified for instance in 'Dante's Inferno', a pen and wash drawing of 1911, and a 'Reclining Nude', an oil of 1912–13, which won her a prize and now belongs to the Slade.

Carrington's attractive presence, and the originality of her character combined with her talent, earned her the friendship, and in certain cases deeper emotions, of several of her most notable contemporaries, including Edward Wadsworth, Stanley Spencer, William Roberts, Mark Gertler and the Nash brothers. Paul was a fellow student and it was no doubt through him that she came to know John. For the first two or three years there was a thriving and happy friendship between the young John Nash and the young Carrington. On his side it was an intense vividly remembered experience of his early years and even after his marriage he remained very fond of her. They met as often as circumstances allowed and exchanged letters constantly, his often being of formidable length. On her side the relationship was both less intense and enduring. The evidence of the letters strongly suggests that Nash had pursued her with vigour, and with vigour had been repulsed, and that perhaps as a consequence of this her affection somewhat declined. After Nash joined the army

they met but rarely, and when they did and Nash attempted to revive old affections, the occasions were not very happy.

John almost certainly wished to marry her, but although she did eventually marry Ralph Partridge in May 1921 she regarded marriage 'as a sad falling-off from a high ideal and the end of creative life for an artist'. Noel Carrington, who made this observation in one of a number of letters to me written in 1978 and 1979, added that she had 'done her best to convert me to her new creed of free association between the sexes'.

John and Carrington's friendship involved intense interest in each other's work, and it was he who encouraged her to practise watercolour and wood engraving. Her 'Hills in Snow at Hurstbourne Tarrant', a watercolour of 1916, was found attributed to him at the Courtauld Institute, and were it to be included in an exhibition of his work its authenticity would be unlikely to be questioned. Another of Noel Carrington's letters to me, dated 30 December 1979, relates to this:

Carrington (seated, far left) with contemporaries at the Slade. The two women behind her to her left are Barbara Hiles and Dorothy Brett; the men in the foreground include C. R. W. Nevinson, Mark Gertler (with walking stick), Stanley Spencer and Adrian Allinson (with dog).
Reproduced by courtesy of the Tate Gallery Archives

Carrington photographed while she was at the Slade.
Reproduced by courtesy of the Tate Gallery Archives.

It is interesting that the snow scene has been credited to JN. . . . It was he himself who sent me a photo of it having been asked by a dealer, the Rutland Gallery, to confirm it was his as it had been sold as a JN. He remembered the scene well enough to suggest it was Carrington's, which led me to go over and identify the landscape and tell the Gallery, by which time they had sold it to the present owner. She referred to the snow in a letter to Mark Gertler at the time [December 1916] but omitted

to say John Nash had inspired her to try a watercolour, as I am sure he did as I know he stopped at Hurstbourne at least once though I was away at the time.

The cause of the affinity between 'Hills in Snow at Hurstbourne Tarrant' and the work of Nash was more specific than their mutual admiration, as is apparent in yet another letter to me from Noel, dated April 1979 and headed 'Recollections of John Nash', about their relationship:

> . . . In many respects she was influenced by him, not only his introducing her to wood-engraving and fresco, but because they had in common a natural affinity for the English countryside as well as for gardens and flowers. In this respect I think that Nash counteracted the influence of her other Slade friends, Gertler, Nevinson, William Roberts. It happened at a period when she was discovering for herself more exciting landscapes in the Hampshire and Wiltshire downland after being brought up in the flat countryside of Bedford. Her favourite authors became W. H. Hudson, Gilbert White, Cobbett

Hills in Snow at Hurstbourne Tarrant, by Dora Carrington. Watercolour, 21¼″ x 25¼″, dated 1916. This painting reflects the influence which Nash had on Carrington, so much so that it has been attributed to him.
Reproduced by courtesy of Mr Anthony Swiffen

and Richard Jefferies. Her one surviving landscape in watercolour was painted under Nash's influence during his visit to her home. I would ascribe largely to him her belief in a 'natural style' and her explicit antipathy to Cubism and contemporary vogue.

The admiration of John and Carrington for the work of the other found expression in frequent discussion about painting (which as a rule he avoided, preferring to talk of literature, music, weather, and botany) as well as in the many gifts of their work which they made to one another. Their professional relationship was not primarily that of master and student: it was one of equals. 'Hills in Snow at Hurstbourne Tarrant', with its rhythmic composition and austere leafless tress against the snow would indeed have been an improbable creation had she not known him, but her 'Reclining Nude' already referred to is superior to any of his.

John greatly treasured Carrington's numerous letters, tying them up in ribbon. One cannot be certain that after half a century and more (the earliest letters were probably written in 1912, the year they met) a number have not been lost, and the same may be said of his, which would appear by far to have exceeded hers, copious letter-writer though she was. These extracts are revealing of the range of subjects covered in their correspondence, from simple every-day matters to descriptions of landscape or highly personal and emotional thoughts. The first two, for instance, relate humorously to the gift of a silk handkerchief which Carrington made to John shortly after they met.

Iver Heath, Bucks (1912)

I have to thank you for the gift of one of the best, if not quite the best, handkerchiefs in Europe. It is like a fine patterned Turkey rug into which in this case one's [drawing of nose] sinks in ecstatical blowings. But [drawing] I haven't yet dared to use it thus and don't believe I shall, but it will come into the category of 'show' handkerchiefs for is it not written?
'one for blow
and
One for show'
This will amuse you; extract from *Observer* 'So & So's sombre work appears in unfavourable contrast to the *thin conventions & childish trivialities* of Mr John Nash's paintings'. Again this emphasis of 'childish'. Do I appear so very young and what does thin convention mean? It sounds like insufficient clothing. I am glad to be

mentioned. Paul thinks it better to be slanged than not mentioned at all as he is.

To this Carrington replied some time later from her parents' house at 1 Rothsay Gardens, Bedford:

. . . *En passant*, as they say, I must first refer to a previous letter of yours. You weren't supposed to use that handkerchief for a nose-wiper! It was a purely decorative piece for encircling the neck. I trust you have not soiled it with anything so vulgar as a loud and stentorious blow of your nasal appendage. Really, Master Jack, you don't think that handkerchiefs like these grow on gooseberry bushes do you?

The next two letters from Carrington to Nash give some idea as to the frequency with which they wrote and saw each other; both date from 1913:

1 Rothsay Gardens, Bedford

. . . The Slade Dance was good. We wished you would have come. All the same I despise myself horribly for taking so keen a delight in shallow frivolities such as dances, & sweetmeats, but alas! It is a sorry fact. Now, I am once again the persevering student.

The Roman Camp, Callander, N.B.
August 2nd

I am sorry to have been so long answering your letters. But it was such a wacking long one last time that I thought a little rest would be pleasant to you. I will now answer them. I am grieved to hear about your nasal appendage. I trust the operation has restored your nose to its proper dimensions.

How exciting the Pre-Raphaelites being back again.[12] I shall go & see them immediately I get back. Oh isn't The Hireling Shepherd amazing! I really think they got there. Wouldn't you like to do a real picture like that? If this letter is rather bad, you mustn't mind as I am so chock-full of happiness that having to stop still & write about past things, & think of words, is hard. . . .

Lena[13] took me to the top of a high hill and we watched the sun set, & she talks beautifully about things & the country. It is good to be about the fields & trees. One night we stole out of the house . . . when everyone was slumbering and ran barefooted with big leaps across the fields through sleeping cows, till we climbed the slope to a cornfield. The moon was new & shining, & the elms big clumps against the emerald purple grey sky, all the fields were dark green grey. Do you ever go out when everything is over at night? The corn field was greeny purple, and poppies marking dark black-red stains and you grabbed at them, for they seemed only stains on the waving mass of wheat. . . . We go out every day drawing on these big mountains . . . & nobody else to be seen. The whole world was ours . . . But how hard to draw, and when we return at 8 we have astounding dinners. Are you above grub? I hate aesthetic people who pretend not to be interested.

John discussed many things in his letters to Carrington, even, uncharacteristically, painting and the work of other artists, as can be seen in this letter dating from the same period as the previous two:

Wood Lane House, Iver Heath, Bucks

. . . Your letters collected will be an interesting addition to English literature one day. . . . I saw the loan exhibition of Pre-Raphaelite at the Tate the other day. I think that for sheer colouring and detail nothing is more satisfying than 'The Hireling Shepherd' [Holman Hunt] if you know it. And for these qualities and feelings as well 'Christ in the Carpenter's Shop', Rossetti's marvellous pictures – Millais' of Hamlet discovering the madness of Ophelia is also there & Millais' 'Lorenzo & Isabella'. . . .

At more or less the same period a note from Carrington, writing from Clearwell, Portland Avenue, Exmouth, casually introduces the woman whom John was to marry: '. . . I met a girl at Slade who was a great friend of Pellew Harvey. . . . I forget her name. I think she does awfully interesting work herself. She wears glasses . . .'. This was Christine Kühlenthal. The letters at this stage clearly suggest that Carrington may have found John's attention a little too oppressive; this letter from John to her does more than hint at some friction between them:

Wood Lane House, Iver Heath

. . . Your soliloquy on the frailty of man received & filed . . . *Now re* 'Landscape'. I am *overjoyed* to hear that it is finished & *I beg you will let me have it as soon as possible as I am shortly taking my rooms & will need it for decorative purposes.* Please do send it to me & *don't keep it back* because I have disappointed you, for after all, sakes alive! of 'marry came up' I know how to take care of myself don't I? & as I have told you before I know all women are *Artful* & a man who has that only as a firm basis of his opinions towards 'em can't be led

into much trouble, can he? Of course what you say about forgiving me now. It's lucky for me you did remember it because it is very kind of you (this is not meant for sarcasm) but *how* do you like me ha! Young women!! There's the rub! and there is where the grit rubs the toe in shoe if you can answer *that* question your [illegible] . . .!

Carrington had no wish to get involved with John emotionally, and he could expect to have such a letter answered by a jocular dismissal: 'Behold the maid worketh & hath not the time to write unto varlets such as thou . . .'. This was at the period when John had started to exhibit with Paul, and Carrington seems increasingly interested in his painting; after teasing him for being too demanding she writes '. . . but I will pass it over being of a generous and noble disposition. . . . Your pictures were good especially Lee and his model made me laugh. One day

Sheringham
Watercolour, 12½" x 15½", 1914. Nash's landscapes of this period met with a good response when exhibited and won him influential patrons such as Sir Michael Sadler and Sir Edward Marsh.
Photo: Anthony d'Offay

Balaam and the Ass
Ink, crayon and watercolour,
13¼″ x 16″, signed and dated
1914. One of many Biblical
scenes which Nash painted
during this period, perhaps
spurred on by his interest in
the Pre-Raphaelites.
Photo: Anthony d'Offay

I ask politely for a landscape of fields and figures from you
to put on my walls and try to coerce Paul too . . .'. John,
then enjoying the success of his first exhibition with Paul,
which earned him both money and praise, as well as the
patronage of figures such as Edward Marsh and Michael
Sadler, wrote:

And now I will tell you what has been happening, if you
would like to know. Friday Club opened on Saturday.
Alas, the new landscape you liked is sold for 8 gns and a
new oil colour to Eddy Marsh. Organ learning progresses
slowly. You ask how can I play (?) I have first to learn
to play at all . . . I am reading Vasari's *Lives of the Italian
Painters*, a very good book.

Please excuse the hail of letters. We have altered our
minds and are keeping the [Dorien Leigh] Gallery on till
Saturday. Prof. Sadler has bought 3 more of mine and
one of Paul's isn't he a frightfully good man. I long to
tell you all about it, it is so exciting. Paul & I hope to
have a tea party in the gallery before it ends. . . .

The success of the exhibition was such that John financed his visit to Florence out of it. He announced his impending departure in a note to Carrington dating from the beginning of January 1914, headed simply 'New Yearish. The same old place'. In the same letter he also writes of his desire to turn from landscape painting and try his hand at Biblical scenes; perhaps it was this ambition that moved him to praise the Pre-Raphaelites so highly. However, he seemed to have some idea that such a style might not be suited to him: 'My brain is addled & I turn to the Bible, but I fear with not much success, my figure drawing being so queer'. Carrington was full of admiration for his success – John had then just joined the Friday Club and the London Group and was exhibiting in Brighton in 'The Camden Town Group & Others' – as well as envy at his going to Florence:

> You are going to Florence! and you announce it calmly in a word and again you tell me with a coolness only found in the Strand magazines, that Maresco [Pearse] has bought your Gipsies! Try and have a little enthusiasm about it. I know after selling so many pictures it must be hard. But surely one doesn't go to Florence every afternoon?

In the event, when John reached Italy, it was landscape that was his predominant concern, as is apparent from the letter he wrote to Carrington from the Villa le Pergole at Careggi, outside Florence:

> I find it extremely difficult to do landscapes here owing to the entire lack of open country. The mountains are very fine but never appear unless it is very clear. I have only seen them once so far. Michael Angelo's David & Benvenuto Cellini's Perseus & Jupiter colossal statues the first in white marble, the latter two in bronze are very fine in the terrace by the Uffizi. The Ponte Vecchio is also marvellous. When I look back to my journey out here nothing pleased me more than the country between London and Dover. The Channel was in fog. The country between Calais & Paris is monstrous. Part of Switzerland we passed through was marvellous, but so big. Between Milan & Bologna the country is inconceivably dull, miles & miles of perfectly square fields (grass) w. broad ditches full of water and bounded by pollarded willows in endless 'sameness'. . . .

Back in England John and Carrington were to grow apart, separated by, ironically, John's desire for a closer relationship with her, the beginning of the war, and, a year later, the appearance of Lytton Strachey on the scene. The break

was by no means simple or unemotional, as these letters, the first from John to Carrington and the second from her to him, clearly show.

Iver Heath

. . . it seems to me that [if] you can forgive me that one insinuation which you have proved to me to be false we might remain good friends better in fact than before, since we must necessarily know each other's temperament better. It is unnecessary for *me* to say that I like you very much for that you should know, of your [work], as you also know, I can [say] very little. What then can possibly stand between our being friends. I *will* be friends with you.

Tuscan Landscape
Watercolour, 14″ x 14½″, signed and dated 1915. Painted after John's return from his Italian journey in 1914, this picture belonged to his brother Paul.
Collection Victor Batte-Laye Trust, The Minories, Colchester

37

Clearwell, Parkland Avenue, Exmouth

Thank you very much for your letter. I am sorry not to have written before as excuses are first cousins to lies & often near relations . . . I will make none & proceed forthwith. Thank you very much for seeing my point of view. You know I would like to be friends with you & if as a friend, I can ever help you I will be happy. You cannot think what pleasure it will give me to know you better. . . .

That such a compromise might last was too much to be hoped; two years later, in 1916, John wrote to Carrington:

. . . I find it terribly difficult to explain to you. I must own I am sceptical about platonic friendship unless each person is as it were sexless but I am not so & my nature is not adapted for it to my mind. I look forward naturally to it . . . meeting someone who would be a friend & more to me. I am always, perhaps foolishly, building castles in the air. I cannot but admire the sureness with which you express yourself so well. I feel you know yourself so well. You are eminently sensible & I will try to be so too now that I know your views, but I beg we may be friends, not acquaintances in future; for now that I have lost a vague possibility if ever there was one of your being more than a friend, surely I must not lose your friendship altogether. You are stronger than me, less affectionate in mind & more independent by virtue of your nature. I feel independence in one's work & life is one of the greatest things. And now I can say no more because it is too hard to think of much. I am afraid to have expressed myself very badly. I must also again ask your pardon for disturbing your peace of mind in any way. . . .

The tone of this letter is markedly more reserved than those of earlier years. One of the main events to come between them had been the war; as John wrote soon after he became a wartime Special Constable in 1914, 'If I was free of family ties I would like to be with you in Wales or some wild remote spot & forget it all. Not that one wishes to fly from any duties that may arise or could despise & think it trivial, but anything for peace. I wish it more a day of miracles & that God would strike down all peacebreakers . . .'.

However, the event which brought their affair to a complete end was Carrington's meeting with Lytton Strachey in 1915. She soon fell deeply in love with him, and spent the rest of her life with him. John seems to have realised immediately the consequences of her meeting with Strachey, writing in 1915:

> . . . I like *you* better than anyone else I know (of womankind) & wd gladly go to Timbuctoo with you but as that can't be I must be patient & wait for someone else to like me. It seems foolish but these times make one need someone close to one in affection & acquaintance & yet I shd almost fear to have another 'affair' so called in case I bungled again.

In the event John easily overcame this fear of becoming involved again; shortly afterwards, in 1916, he wrote to Carrington from Iver Heath:

> I have been seeing a lot of Christine and we had very jolly expeditions: to Jordans among other places. . . . You do not know Christine so well as I do. I have taken more trouble & patience to 'unravel' her as you say I don't wish to brag about it over you because she really unravelled herself to me, indeed probing is little more than questions & answers, if the former is evaded the probe can't do its work. . . . I would like to know Strachey. I have always been repelled by his outward appearance. . . . Yes, Christine is a rare creature. You use an apt expression . . .
>
> P.S. Christine & I love each other. Please write to me.

Even after his marriage to Christine John continued to hope for a special relationship with Carrington; the letter in which he announces his wedding, however, reflects the continuing friction between them:

> c/o Mrs Wheeler, Horn Hill Rd, Chalfont St Peter, Bucks
>
> I think we will not continue the arguments. It is neither seemly nor proper that friends of such long & excellent standing should toss a heavy & prickly ball about from hand to hand. I am sure you will at least credit me w. sincerity of feeling in writing what I did even you will not believe me when I said I liked Lytton I am now going to bury the bone of contention: let no roving jackal disinter [it] from its resting place. Now you shall know I am wedded and bedded & on this head I expect a storm to break on me for not having written before. Christine & I have just settled down at the above address. Paul lives just down the road in a good farm & [we] are both in a large room for our bloody war pictures. . . .

John continued to write to Carrington, but an element of self-consciousness appears in his letters, which in the long term probably served to inhibit and end their correspondence. For instance, referring to Lytton Strachey's *Eminent Victorians* he writes:

> Lytton has a fine satire at his command I am not clear at expressing my feelings for the craftsmanship itself & I fear to appear like a cheap reviewer. You will understand that when I say it *is* a good book. . . . Perhaps this does not interest you & you will say I am insincere. Hy, young woman speak up!! . . .

They saw each other and corresponded less and less often; when they did meet the occasion was apt to be neither happy nor relaxed. In 1924, writing from Ham Spray, where she had just moved to with Lytton Strachey and her husband Ralph Partridge, Carrington wrote of a visit:

> I am sorry you didn't enjoy your visit more. For with my penetrating eye (& ear) I saw you didn't. . . . To tell the truth I thought you seemed rather sad, but perhaps it was only my depressing effect and the catarrh. I hope so, I mean that you are gay & happy in general. . . . You are an owl to think I minded your reference to my private affairs. It was nice of you to sympathise. Although to tell you the truth I am so happy in this Paradise with my cat, that I hardly mind now. . . .

From this time on they rarely saw each other; John caught sight of Carrington once in Bath in the September of 1926, and his memories stirred, he wrote to her proposing that he should visit, 'for blood is thicker than petrol or petrol as thick as blood so I *shd.* like to see you again & see what you look like hence this letter'. It is not known whether this resulted in any meeting; but by this time their relationship was one of mere acquaintances.

In 1931 Lytton Strachey, who had made her life worth living, was afflicted by the cancer of which he was to die. When the end was clearly inevitable she attempted to take her own life. Not long afterwards she made a further attempt, and she died at the age of thirty-eight. Not long before, she wrote, quoting from Sir Henry Wooton, lines he had written in 1627:

> *He first deceased she for*
> *a little tried*
> *to live without him. Liked*
> *it not and died.*

CHAPTER IV
The First World War

Just before the outbreak of the war Paul and John took a holiday together, visiting Paul's close friends Gordon and Emily Bottomley at Silverdale in the Lake District. On their way back war was declared, but they called on Michael Sadler in Leeds and stayed with my father's elder brother Charles Rutherston in Bradford – two of John's extremely rare visits to art collectors.

During the autumn of 1914 the brothers worked as agricultural labourers, harvesting in Dorset. On 14 October John was sworn in as a Special Constable for Buckingham. He moved to London early in 1915 and took a room in Marchmont Street, opposite Russell Square tube station, in order to work at making army tents at Mappin & Webb. Evenings were spent in avant-garde circles at the Café

Dorset Landscape
Chalk and wash, 16¼" x 15¼", c.1915. Drawn while Nash was engaged in an abortive project to decorate the village hall at Bryantspuddle, the assurance and sophistication of this view shows how fast his skills as an artist developed.
Trustees of the Tate Gallery, London

Royal, but his room was twice infested by insects and he returned briefly to Iver Heath. In February 1916, having been rejected by the army, he took a clerical post with the Ministry of Munitions in Northumberland Avenue, often staying with Sir Edward Marsh, who was then Private Secretary to Winston Churchill. In September 1916 he was able to enlist in The Artists' Rifles, the 28th London Regiment, serving in France from November of that year until January 1918.

As it was for most of those who served in the army, the war was for John a horrific experience. The Artists' Rifles, in which there were a number of under-age recruits, was an Officers' Training Corps. In spite of its name it was a regiment in which almost no artists were serving, but several musicians. After the completion of a course at Oppy Wood, on the Belgian Front, in June 1917, John was made a Lance-Corporal being put through severe tests to ascertain whether his courage and endurance justified his promotion. Before long he was made a full Corporal, and eventually a Sergeant, which oddly enough, he appears not to have known until he returned to England.

Trench Mortar Firing at Evening
Watercolour, 14" x 11¼", c.1918. Like many artists of his generation, the impact of life in the trenches had an immediate effect on Nash's style.
Trustees of the Imperial War Museum, London

42

'Roland trying to undo bomb the wrong way after doubting my knowledge of the job. . .' Drawing from an undated letter from John to Paul, probably written while John was on a trench mortar course at Houdkerk in 1917.
Photo: Royal Academy of Arts

The sector in which they received their training was supposed to be a quiet one; it proved, however, otherwise, and shells fell frequently. One, he recalled, 'landed on a trench and there was a terrible mess'; he saw 'sandbags full of remains of men; one became callous and hardened to these sights', and once he and his friends were shelled by their own artillery. He also recalled 'eating one's bully beef among dead men without bothering'[14]. Then, in June 1917, the unit was sent suddenly into the front line.

Before 'going over the top', John held several advance posts beyond the front line, accompanied by two men to keep watch and another to keep in touch with their forward trenches, returning before daybreak. One night the forward party was larger than usual and commanded by an officer who had a premonition of his own death; he was killed on 30 December 1917.

Nash only spent about three weeks in the front line, but during that time went over the top several times, at Cambrai, Marcoing and elsewhere. It was a period, however brief, of unforgettably exacting and fearful experience. 'We were training near Houdkerk for Passchendaele' he said, and when asked if he took part in that battle he replied: 'No. I was lucky. . . . But I remember going to my commanding officer . . . and asking rather indignantly why I wasn't allowed to go up. . . . He said "it's no reflection on your courage. But we can't have all our N.C.O.s killed. We have to keep a certain number back". And then instead of going up there [where] one was certain to be maimed or killed, I was sent on this trench mortar course. I went . . . all over the place, every kind of mortar, big ones to the smallest. . . . I was seconded or attached to the trench-mortar battery and knew all about it but never took it into action. . . . I was a sort of bomb expert. . . . I knew all about bombs. I had a little book with very careful illustrations I made, I may have got it still, all carefully drawn out of all the English bombs and the German bombs'.[15]

As the months passed he became increasingly frustrated at not being given a commission; a man of education and courage, who had moreover applied himself with enthusiasm to an important aspect of trench warfare. In at least three letters to Christine Kühlenthal he expressed his frustration: 'I have just made a bid for a commission in the R[oyal] E[ngineers] as my uncle Hugh Jackson has offered to help me', he wrote on 3 May 1917. 'He is C.O. of the 2nd Labour Battn out there. I don't really know if there is the slightest hope of it. You see, my love, time draws upon us when I must be thinking about a commission, though as yet no one has asked me and I have said I am not in a hurry for one. If this fails there is a chance of getting into the machine-gun section. Anything but Infantry seems the general cry here now. However I must wait and look after myself when the time comes . . .'. But the lack of progress intensified his frustration, and on 28 July 1917 he wrote: '. . . Why shd shop walkers and grocers get commissions and I, at any rate a public school man – a silly social fact that counts much in the army – have to live in dugouts, eating crudely, living scarcely more decently than a beast . . .'.

In a letter dated 27 November, but begun on 20 November 1917 he wrote: '. . . Paul had a talk w. my C.O. who led [him] to suppose that there were still some people before me to go & said I shd be far better as an instructor in a specialist job – P said he was very decent in speaking of me & offered to recommend me highly if anyone asked for me . . .'.

Evidently nothing resulted from this talk. John's failure in the face of his repeated attempts throughout that year to secure a commission is very strange, especially in view of the appalling number of casualties, and of his practical intelligence. Paul always tried to keep in touch with him and where possible help him, as this letter he wrote to his wife Margaret on 5 November 1917 from Intelligence H.Q. suggests:

I waited also until I could see Jack and give you news of him. Whatever powers work for good and mercy have indeed favoured our little family. I must not say much

but I can tell you that Jack has been miraculously spared
in that he did not go over this time as he was kept back
as he is a very useful man. I found the dear old fellow at
last after a day's search looking very well – a bronzed
and tattered soldier, with incredible hands overgrown
with cuticle – his eyes I thought less shy, very blue, and
bright, thin in the face; his voice rather tired, but giving

out the same wit and humour as of old. He was very happy and though I listened with horror and wonder to all he had seen and felt, he seemed to have been only tremendously interested, enjoying the humorous things that had happened. He confesses the sight of wounded and dying men unnerved him. At present he's on a trench mortar course far behind the lines, where he will be for a fortnight. After that time he may go for a rest – there are so few left, I should think it unlikely he will go up the line yet. We had a jolly day together it being Sunday so he was free – motoring through the pleasant lands of France. I am going to try and push on his course by seeing his Company Commander. [16]

The possibility of John becoming a war artist had evidently been talked of for some considerable time. It is referred to in a letter from Carrington to her brother Noel, which he recalls as having been written in 1917 when he was stationed in Rouen, where, by chance, he had met Paul. This, as usual with her letters, undated, runs in part:

Jack Nash has been home on leave. I stayed on my way up to London at that curious house of theirs at Iver Heath. Jack seemed rather nervy. He has been having a very bad time of it and nearly all his company was killed. Paul Nash talked a great deal about you. Evidently you made a very favourable impression! But I like Jack Nash much better. I think he may get one of those artist's jobs and so get transferred home. I hope so. He deserves it more than Nevinson or Paul Nash.

It is strange that such a crucial matter does not appear to have been mentioned in any of John's letters.

Help came, however, from a more purposeful and influential quarter than John's Company Commander, who in any case had only referred to 'recommending him highly' in a vague sense. Paul appealed to Sir Edward Marsh, writing early in 1918 'Can you by any fair or foul means help Jack home for a commission? . . . It is unnecessary to speak of Jack's worth and his real value as an English artist and it's a damned shame if nothing can be done to extricate him from a position in which he is in utmost danger'. In a further letter of 8 January 1918 Paul added 'All my own success and happiness turns bitter when I think of Jack in the trenches'. [17]

John in fact returned to England later that month when a singular incident occurred before he was demobilised. One day, walking in the street, although in uniform, he was arrested as a deserter by a sergeant. He rather enjoyed the fuss arising from the administrative error. When it was discovered he was, of course, promptly released. On 27 February 1918 he was officially demobilised.

In the meantime Marsh exerted his influence and on 3 May 1918 John was commissioned as an honorary Second Lieutenant in the 2nd Battalion of the Artists' Rifles. This enabled him to draw army pay and be provided with a uniform so that he could revisit the Western Front; in the event, when this opportunity arose in November 1918 he turned it down, preferring to carry out his work at home, especially as one of the most important paintings, 'Oppy Wood', was already squared up. He worked on instructions from the War Office for the Ministry of Information, and later for the Imperial War Museum, which now houses twenty-eight paintings and drawings based on his experiences on active service during the First World War.

In order to carry out these paintings John, as did Paul, required a studio. As they had been separated for so long they wished to be together; they rented a large shed, formerly used for herb-drying, at Chalfont St Peter near Gerrard's Cross. Here they settled in early June 1918. As it proved to be exceedingly uncomfortable they found bearable living quarters nearby, but continued to work and eat in the shed. Paul described something of their lives there in a letter of 16 July 1918 to Gordon Bottomley:

> . . . It is a roomy place with large windows down both sides, an ample studio – here we work. Jack is lately married – a charming girl whom we all adore . . . they live in rooms in a little house next the shed and Bunty [Margaret, Paul's wife] and I have a room in the old farm. . . . We all lunch together in the studio where there is a piano so our wives enchant us with music thro' the day. A phantastic existence as all lives seem these days but good while it lasts and should produce something worthwhile I suppose. France and the trenches would be a mere dream I suppose if our minds were not perpetually bent upon those scenes. . . .[18]

Paul's expectation that their 'phantastic existence' at Chalfont 'should produce something worthwhile' was amply fulfilled. It was there that he began one of his most notable paintings, 'The Menin Road', completed the following year and now in the Imperial War Museum. But for John it was even more worthwhile, for there he made two oil paintings, widely different in character but both of a rare impressiveness. These are 'Over the Top: 1st Artists' Rifles at Marcoing, 30 December, 1917' and 'Oppy Wood, 1917, Evening', also in the Museum.

In a letter of 15 January 1974 to Joseph Darracott,

Keeper, Art and Design History at the Imperial War Museum, John described the events represented in and related to 'Over the Top', one of the few paintings by an official artist of a specific military action in the First World War. He retained vivid memories of it.

The attack in daylight in the snow by B. Com. in which I was then a Sergeant was designed as a diversion to a bombing raid up a support trench on the left. We were supposed to be supported by A Com. following on, but they were withdrawn. We never got to grips with the enemy but were stopped in sight of them. We had to 'hole up' in craters and shell holes till nightfall and then got back to our original line. Casualties were very heavy. All officers killed or wounded and only one Sergeant left, and the Q.M.S. It was in fact pure murder and I was lucky to escape untouched. So you see I have very special memories as I was in charge of about fourteen men of the Bomber section. . . . It was bitterly cold and we were easy targets against the snow and in daylight. . . . I think the vivid memory of the occasion helped me when I painted the picture and provoked whatever intensity of feeling may be found in it. . . .

In a conversation with Darracott and his colleague David Brown on 4 March 1974 John Nash recalled that on his way to the front line before going over the top he was wearing a new coat with sergeant's stripes. (His memory was at fault; he was still a corporal.) Thinking that they were conspicuous he left the coat behind and went into action wearing an old tunic. He felt very cold. Before the action he was shown a map and given only vague indications of where he and the others should make for. The Colonel commanded 'Over the Top' and the soldiers climbed out of the trench. Nash tried to make the men avoid bunching together. 'There was not a shot for a while, suddenly the Germans opened up and that seemed to be every machine gun in Europe.' Finally they stopped running and could see the helmets of the enemy. These events occurred at about 11 am and later in the day a British plane flew over to see what had happened,

One of the men in the regiment wrote an account of the action signed 'R.A.L.' (R. A. Lee, a sergeant in the Headquarters Wing of the 1st Battalion, Artists' Rifles). It reads in part:

The picture 'Over the Top' has always been of particular interest to me because the first time I saw it, some years after Nash painted it, it immediately recalled in every detail the early morning scene at Welsh Ridge on December 30th, 1917. . . .

. . . Just before daybreak on December 30th the Germans – taking advantage of the mist – launched an

Stand To Before Dawn
Pen and watercolour, 13″ x 15½″, c.1918. This vividly evokes the hours of waiting before the order to 'go over the top' was given.
Trustees of the Imperial War Museum, London

The Menin Road
Painted by Paul Nash while he was sharing the studio with John at Chalfont St Peter in 1919, this view shows a certain similarity to the latter's *Oppy Wood*. Oil on canvas, 72″ x 125″.
Trustees of the Imperial War Museum, London

attack, capturing most of the positions which had been held by the Regiment up till the previous night. As a result of this, the Regiment was called upon to deliver a counter attack and recapture the lost positions. The attacking Companies were 'A' and 'B' with 'D' in support and 'C' in reserve.

. . . the Regiment moved up the front line, which may sound quite an easy operation today, but which was actually – owing to the fatigued condition of many of the troops, and the difficulty in making reasonable progress owing to the frozen state of the trenches and obstructions in the said trenches caused by casualties, also heavy shelling – a very tedious and trying movement. As a matter of fact the move was so slow that my own Company ('B') only arrived in the front line at zero hour and had to jump out 'Over the Top' immediately on arrival. This is what you can actually see in Nash's picture! The snow and mist; men of 'B' Company characterised by the blue square on the upper arm of their greatcoats; the sergeant with a Lewis gun, already the sole survivor of his Lewis-gun section, and later a casualty himself. . . .[19]

I would be reluctant to criticise the aesthetic qualities of 'Over the Top', a representation of an action in which the artist took part and so deeply moved a fellow participant as well as others who had experienced actions of a comparable character. Fortunately the dignity, the energy, above all the grim harmony with which this tragic event is depicted renders criticism needless. It is a memorable achievement, especially by a self-taught artist who had only begun to paint a few years earlier and while on active service was unable to continue. 'I had very little to go on except my memory', Nash said in a sound record made by the Imperial War Museum; 'I think I did make a few notes, possibly on letters I had in my pocket. You see drawing wouldn't have been encouraged by [the] Commanding Officer or anyone in the line. You might have been taken for a spy'[20]. (Elsewhere he alluded to having made rather more elaborate sketches, and he said to me 'behind the lines I did some pure landscape. It was a means of saving my life'.)

'Over the Top' is an acknowledged masterpiece. Of its outstanding qualities the most significant is the way in which the figures advancing over the snow appear, except for the front four who are in line, so various in posture. Four lie dead, others scramble out of the trench, yet the composition is classical, the distant end of the trench meeting that of the advancing line and making the remote hinge which affords a point of unity to these tragic figures and their environment. The picture is remarkable, too, in that a painter who so rarely painted figures should have portrayed these with such command.

Nash's time in the shed at Chalfont was very productive. Besides 'Over the Top' he painted, as noted, 'Oppy Wood' (the largest of his war paintings, measuring 72″ × 84″) a work comparable in-quality with 'Over the Top'. Yet in spite of the devastation represented, in spirit 'Oppy Wood' is a peace rather than a war picture. Neither for dramatic intensity nor for insight into war does it compare with 'Over the Top'. The ground in the front of the trench is indeed shell-pitted, the blasted trees have no branches, yet a great quiet suffuses the scene, a quiet so potent as to still the sound of the explosions of two shells away on the left, a quiet that seems the harbinger of the greater quiet that will still the sound of all the guns, of the return of sanity, that will allow gardening and botany to resume their places among the pursuits of man.

Besides these two major works he painted 'The Cornfield'. About this he wrote to the Tate on 7 July 1952 after its bequest by Sir Edward Marsh through the Contemporary Art Society that year: 'I remember we were very punctilious about working for the Ministry of Information all day and did not allow ourselves to do any of our own peacetime work until after 6 o'c in the evenings! This was the first painting (not war) that I did after being released from the Army'. That year he also made a watercolour

study of the same subject from a different angle, which came to the Tate as part of the same bequest.

John gave a slightly fuller account, in *Artists in an Age of Conflict*[21], of how he decided to paint his first 'peacetime' subject:

> My brother was very punctilious . . . he wouldn't do any of his own work or allow me to do any, until the strain became too much doing nothing but war paintings. And as the summer came he made a rule that after six o'clock we should allow ourselves to walk out on the landscape and perhaps do a peacetime landscape and forget the war paintings. And I know quite well that's how I came to paint that Cornfield . . . in the Tate. Of course, I did it from a place nearby. . . .

John's post-war paintings showed a marked difference from his earlier works, with their slightly primitive, naïve appearance. With 'Over the Top', 'Oppy Wood' and 'The Cornfield' he had reached his full maturity.

Oppy Wood, 1917, Evening
Oil on canvas, 72" x 84", 1918. Perhaps the most impressive of all Nash's war paintings.
Trustees of the Imperial War Museum, London

CHAPTER V

Marriage and the Post-War Years

While John was completing his commissions as a war artist, he was also settling back into normal civilian life. As mentioned in the preceding chapter, after his return from France he was married to Christine Kühlenthal. Christine was the daughter of Wilhelm Heinrich Kühlenthal, son of Carl Kühlenthal. Wilhelm was born in Xanten, in the Rhineland, on 27 May 1863. He emigrated to England to work as a chemist, marrying a Scottish girl, Ada Josephine Bustin, in 1891. Christine was born on 11 January 1895 at Krishna Villa, Pinner Road, Harrow.

She and John were married in May 1918, the ceremony being conducted by the Reverend George Culshaw of the Rectory, Iver Heath. Harry Nash was his friend and churchwarden, Gilbert Spencer was best man, a role which John himself was to take on when Gilbert married Ursula Bradshaw in 1930; they used to joke about the way both of them were overshadowed by their elder brothers.

Christine proved a dedicated wife. Their profuse correspondence shows that after their engagement, while he was still at the front, she assiduously looked after his professional affairs, arranging for the exhibition and sale of his works, providing him with drawing materials, as well as raising money on his behalf. At the same time she was teaching painting at Roger Fry's Omega Workshops and at the Arts & Crafts, giving music lessons and engaging in various other activities. In the early days of their marriage she felt frustrated by the difficulty of reconciling her desire to resume painting with her devotion to John, a demanding husband. But this quickly passed and she showed her devotion in every possible way. She withheld facts liable to disturb his peace of mind: assumed complete responsibility for his financial affairs, for his health (apart from the fact that, like her, he was a heavy smoker) and mended his

clothes. Moreover, she chose, precisely, landscapes for him to represent, often going to explore some distant place in which he had expressed interest.

Shortly after their marriage they travelled to Bavaria to visit some relatives of Christine's father. From Tüfzing, Sternberg See, Munich, he wrote Paul one of the rare letters in which he referred to paintings:

> We went yesterday to the Alte Pinacothek in Munich and saw all the German Primitives. Altdorfer most fine, Durer etc. Rooms of fleshy Rubens some very wonderful. 2 excellent El Grecos and some lovely Poussins. There are no English pictures. Rembrandt is well represented tho'. We also visited the State Gallery of Modern Work, quite one of the best collections I've seen. Van Gogh and Self Portrait are wonderful there were some very interesting modern German and Russian. And then . . . we entered the New Pinacothek Gallery, equivalent to our Tate. Never go there if you can help it. It is no exaggeration to say there is *not one* work of art there – 100 times worse than Millbank at its worst period, sickening Overbakian trash!!!

John was always an extremely prolific letter writer and it would be absurd for me to claim to have read more than a

John, Paul and Christine Kühlenthal at Gerrards Cross. John's sergeant's stripes suggests that the photograph was taken early in 1918, before he received his commission as a war artist in May that year.
Collection Ronald Blythe
Left: *The Artist's Wife* Christine drawn by John in 1920. Pencil, 14¾″ x 10¾″, signed and dated.
Photo: Royal Academy of Arts

relatively small proportion of his correspondence, but I have never read one of his letters in which he referred to so many paintings, at which, except for those of his brother and friends, he was usually reluctant even to look. (This was also invariably true of architecture, churches in particular, which he pointedly ignored.)

Back in England John's friendship with Sir Edward Marsh continued to develop. He bought 'The Cornfield' from John soon after it was completed, and in 1919 gave it to Ivor Novello, one of his most intimate friends, on condition that he bequeath it to the Contemporary Art Society for eventual presentation to the Tate. Novello died a year before Marsh, to whom it was returned, and he himself fulfilled his original condition. He expressed, more than once, his ardent admiration for it. Indeed with what glowing dignity this work, so simple in its design, held its place on the walls of Marsh's rooms at 5 Raymond Buildings, Gray's Inn. These became ever more crowded with perceptively chosen works, almost all by young contemporaries. 'Every available inch was occupied', observed Paul, 'Pictures began in the hall, ran up the stairs, along passages and were only pulled up by the bathroom'.

It is not often that artists respond to the generous encouragement of collectors of their work with so large and impressive a tribute as they did to Eddie in the exhibition 'An Honest Patron: A Tribute to Sir Edward Marsh', sponsored by *The Liverpool Daily Post* and the Bluecoat Gallery, Liverpool, in 1976. John, by way of an introduction to the catalogue, wrote the following reminiscences:

Eddie Marsh must have been one of my earliest patrons, as he was to so many young artists. I do not think his means were ample and he must have scrapped his income to buy what his taste and enthusiasm drove him to acquire. I believe he received occasional windfalls from vague relations and these he turned into account in his patronage. His hospitality chiefly consisted in putting one up for the night or asking one to breakfast. I used to sleep in a narrow bed in one of the smaller rooms in his quarters at Raymond Buildings, and just above me and threatening, as I thought, to fall on me was Stanley Spencer's large painting 'Apple Gatherers' (which Marsh presented to the Tate in 1946). The walls everywhere were plastered with pictures and even the doors had to share in supporting his collection. As one was leisurely breakfasting E. M. would be preparing to leave for the Colonial Office and on his way downstairs would shout or scream in his high-pitched voice a series of instructions

to his housekeeper Mrs Elgy. He placed great trust in this valued factotum. 'Mrs E.' he would say, 'ring the Prime Minister's Secretary and tell him etc. etc.' and 'Mrs E. ring up . . .' some other important personality. To all this, as he clattered downstairs, came the calm reply 'Yes, Mr Marsh, yes, Mr Marsh'. Later one heard her carrying out his numerous orders which, considering she was rather deaf, seemed quite an achievement. . . .

He was always trying to help young and struggling artists either by direct help or introduction to other patrons. When one stayed with him one got some idea of his current enthusiasm – he might be playing Patience of an evening or teaching himself to read music. These visits afforded one a bed for the night – very helpful to an artist living as I did in the country – as well as providing the enjoyment of his company. In appearance E. M. was very neat and dapper and the monocle under

The Cornfield 1918
Oil on canvas, 27″ x 30″.
Nash's first major post-war work. While the abstract structure of this landscape is handled far more decisively, in other respects the subject is closely related to *Gloucestershire Landscape* (1914; page 24)
Right: *The Cornfield* Watercolour, 7¼″ x 10½″, 1918. This study shows another view of the same field.
Trustees of the Tate Gallery, London

Above: *Cornfields, Wiston,*
Suffolk

Oil on canvas, 22″ x 30″,
c.1935.

One of Nash's favourite
subjects.

his up-twisted eyebrow gave him an added distinction. Scholar, Civil Servant, Patron of the Arts, his enthusiasm pervaded all branches.

In the same introduction John recalled weekends spent with Eddie's boss at the Colonial Office, Malcolm MacDonald, who would often entertain at his country house near Chelmsford, inviting at Eddie's suggestion other young artists such as Gilbert Spencer.

John and Christine remained at Chalfont St Peter until the autumn of 1919 when they settled at Gerrard's Cross in a flat over a chemist's shop, spending their first summer at nearby Whiteleaf, Princes Risborough and the second at Sapperton in Gloucestershire.

While living at Gerrard's Cross he was versatile in his activities. It was during this period that he began his extensive work as a book illustrator. However, most of his time he devoted to painting, establishing a place for himself among the talented young artists then working in England. As such he was invited to take part in a scheme set up by Sir Michael Sadler, Vice-Chancellor of the University of Leeds and a collector who already knew John's work, to make designs for panels for Leeds Town Hall. In this he was assisted by William Rothenstein. The other artists taking part were Paul Nash, Edward Wadsworth, Stanley Spencer, H. S. Williamson, Jacob Kramer and Rothenstein's brother Albert Rutherston.

The scheme was to be a melancholy failure, largely through the incompatibility of the artists involved; although my father was an admirer of Stanley Spencer's work, he felt bound to reject his designs as ill-adapted to the others. In a letter to John, Paul described both how Stanley Spencer angered William Rothenstein by 'protesting against his designs being inspected by a committee', and also how he jeopardised the project for the other artists.

. . . he did accept to work with five other artists under certain conditions nor did he raise any more objections at a subsequent meeting therefore the scheme went forward. Now by his stupid action he has let us all down & hung up the scheme. This is certainly not what [Desmond] Coke wd call in the Public School Tradition nor is it 'cricket' so called nor is it anything but bloody nonsensical arrogance on the part of a very young man who has become enlarged in the headpiece. However that may be, Spencer has not fulfilled his undertaking inspite of [illegible] to do so, Albert, Wadders [Wadsworth] & self feel this shd be pointed out to S. Spencer in no uncertain terms showing disapproval simply as a body of

colleagues & we want you to add your name to a letter which will be submitted to all. At first I was not for it but thinking it over & realising the attitude S.S. is now sure to take up I think Will shd be supported & S.S. made to feel that we resent his actions as artists whom he has chosen to disregard as colleagues.

Millworkers Landscape
Nash's projected design for panels for Leeds Town Hall, which were never actually made.
Leeds City Art Gallery/Photo: Courtauld Institute of Art, University of London

Sadler was disappointed, and the attitude of the municipal authorities wholly negative, so it was agreed to let the matter quietly drop. The designs were eventually presented to the British Museum. I remember how severely my father blamed himself for his support for a project so unlikely to be realised and the failure of which caused distress to several painters whom he both liked and admired. The municipal attitude does not surprise me in view of the fact that Sadler, owner, beyond comparison, of the finest collection of modern art in Leeds was never invited to become a member of the art galleries committee.

For John, however, the Leeds project was only a small setback during a period when his work as an illustrator and landscape painter was fast achieving recognition. In 1921 he held his first one-man exhibition in London at the Goupil Gallery, the success of which amply justified the post-war career he had chosen.

CHAPTER VI
Book Illustrator

As mentioned in the previous chapter, it was during this period that John Nash began his work as a book illustrator, for which he is perhaps most highly regarded today. In 1919 he illustrated a book which became a classic, *Dressing Gowns and Glue* by Lance Sieveking, providing the frontispiece, title page, vignette, fifteen line drawings in the text and illustrations on both covers. An introduction to the verses was written by G. K. Chesterton, the drawings were introduced by Max Beerbohm, and there was a general introduction by Cecil Palmer, who also, with Paul, served as editor. The book was the first of no less than forty-seven books illustrated by John entirely or in part, until almost the end of his life.

These books are notable achievements in themselves and like his drawings in general, had an intensifying effect on his painting both in oil and watercolour. He was at his finest when he depicted pure landscape, often cultivated fields of corn, woods, streams and ponds, either without human figures or if they were included placed subordinately. His drawings from his schooldays onwards and the evidence of those who knew him testify to his fascination with his fellow men and women; had he not frequently drawn them he would surely have been tempted to introduce them into his landscapes, which owe much of their character to being pure landscapes, rather than scenes in which the presence of the human figure is liable to attract the prime attention of the spectator.

Thus he was able to express his response to harmonious landscape as well as to the human comedy, so that one never impinged upon the other. In his introduction to the drawings in *Dressing Gowns and Glue*, Max Beerbohm – who better qualified? – describes the character of this feature of his art.

That a comic drawing should itself be comic seems to be a reasonable demand. Yet it is a demand which few comic

Opposite
Above: *Landscape near Princes Risborough*
Oil on canvas. Dating from the late 1920s, this view looking towards the Chiltern Hills is based on sketches made within half a mile of Nash's home at Meadle.

Below: *Wormingford Mill Pond*
Black chalk and watercolour, 10¾″ x 15″, c.1922. Nash returned often to this scene, particularly in later life when he went to live near Wormingford at Bottengoms Farm.
Photo: Blond Fine Art

draughtsmen meet. Comic drawings for the most part are but comic ideas seriously illustrated. . . . Even in serious art the labour should not be obtruded on us. In comic art it is fatal. Lightness, an air of take-it-or-leave-it spontaneity, is needed to conserve fun. Nor is this all. A light, cursory method is not inconsistent with realism. It may suggest men and things precisely as they are. That is not fatal; but it is undesirable. What we want, and what John Nash very signally has, is a light method that is extravagant, that is absurd, a method ancillary to a visitation of the world not as (at an earnest glance) the world is, but as, for two pins, one fine morning, it might be, inasmuch that the absurdities inherent in even the best of us could no longer be hushed up.

This view was shared by Douglas Percy Bliss, painter, illustrator and one-time director of the Glasgow School of Art, who wrote in his *History of Wood Engraving* that John's 'sense of humour . . . enables him *to make the best comic drawings of today*'. This opinion is disputable but it is that of a responsible artist-critic, and John's comic drawings occupy a high place. His mastery of facial expression and gesture – especially when he depicted whole groups of characters – was already apparent in *Dressing Gowns and Glue*, and was to remain with him throughout his life, notably in *The Natural History of Selborne* published by the Limited Editions Club in 1972. Of the regular contributors to *Punch* John wrote in an article for the *The London Mercury* in November 1928: 'Very little need be said, but what a relief it would be if one week *Punch* went mad and appeared upside down or, better still, no print at all, and if all the artists gave free rein to whatever absurdity possesses them that week'.

John's sense of humour was at times irrepressible, occurring most spontaneously in the many drawings with which he illustrated his correspondence. Almost every one of his letters to Carrington was embellished by a comic drawing or visual pun, sometimes elaborate, sometimes very slight; there are also many amusing illustrations in his letters to Paul as well as Paul's to him. However not all his correspondence is illustrated; few, for instance, of his letters to Christine, and least of all those written from the front, where drawings would have been liable to provoke trouble with the censor.

In his illustrations his humour is most apparent in, for instance, the rapt attention with which a group of dull, elderly men focus on a commonplace dancing woman showing off her commonplace leg; this drawing, together

with another, even wittier, entitled 'La Boutique Fantasque', accompanied a review of *The Belle of New York* published in *Land and Water* in 1919. The latter is masterly in that it represents six figures, each one distinct in expression and gesture (except for a somewhat anonymous lady in the background).

John's versatility as an illustrator found expression in various media. In 1921 he became one of the early members of the Society of Wood Engravers, which had been founded the year before by a circle of artists which included Edward Gordon Craig, Lucien Pissarro and Eric Gill. During this period John was commissioned to do a number of wood engravings for periodicals; one such was *Land and Water* on which he served as art critic and illustrator for theatre reviews.

In the meantime *Dressing Gowns and Glue* was followed by *The Sun Calendar*, published in 1920, to which both brothers and Rupert Lee contributed illustrations. This was followed by *The Nouveau Poor*, by Belinda Blinders (the pseudonym of Desmond Coke, a friend of John's and collector of his work). This appeared in 1921 and was illustrated entirely by John. These three works, except for a

'Quiet Evening'. Wood engraving c.1924 showing John's wife Christine and his sister Barbara at Lane End House, Meadle. The breadth of the cutting is characteristic of his style.
Collection: Victor Batte-Laye Trust, The Minories, Colchester

'Our heroine's indomitable brightness even at breakfast'. Illustration from *The Nouveau Poor* by Belinda Blinders (Chapman & Hall, 1921). *Collection: Victor Batte-Lay Trust, The Minories, Colchester*

A wood engraving for *Directions to Servants* by Jonathan Swift (Golden Cockerel Press, 1925). *Collection: Victor Batte-Lay Trust, The Minories, Colchester*

woodcut on the wrapper of the second, were illustrated with line-drawings. In 1925 two books appeared, Swift's *Directions to Servants*, which John was invited to illustrate by Robert Gibbings, a neighbour and fellow member of the Society of Wood Engravers, and Ovid's *Elegies* translated by Christopher Marlowe, published together with *The Epigrams of Sir John Davies*. These were the first books he illustrated with wood engravings. The *Epigrams* contains one of the first of his numerous woodcuts of flowers. *Directions to Servants* reveals his sense of humour but neither series has the rhythmic clarity of his finest wood engravings – such as the many he executed for *Poisonous Plants*, his first major commission, published in 1927, and to which he also contributed an introduction.

Of his many illustrated books the last, and among the finest, is the second edition of Gilbert White's *The Natural History of Selborne*, first published in 1951, illustrated with

'I have known a whole village up in arms', from *The Natural History of Selborne* by Gilbert White. This colour lithograph comes from the second edition of the *Natural History* Nash illustrated, published by the Limited Editions Club in 1972. *Collection: Victor Batte-Lay Trust, The Minories, Colchester*

'Thorn Apple'. Wood
engraving from *Poisonous
Plants* (Etchells & Macdonald,
1927).

*Collection: Victor Batte-Lay
Trust, The Minories, Colchester*

line drawings, and brought out again in 1972 with the addition of sixteen colour lithographs (by that time he suffered so acutely from arthritis that he needed help in applying the colour, so after he had made one set of proofs he secured the help of a talented young artist, Pamela Mara to complete the project.) Colour, and the increase in size of the reproductions transformed a notable into an outstanding work. Its thirty-two illustrations include a number of his best, such as 'Well Entertained with a Sunflower', showing a bird pecking at its seeds, 'The Night Jar', another about to catch an insect, a pair of mice nibbling growing wheat, and a wide range of wooded landscapes, some of which, as 'I have known a whole Village up in Arms', include figures.

Unlike several of John's most perceptive admirers I regard his best paintings as his highest achievements, but when I look at the first two of these illustrations, so impressive in their largeness and variety of form, showing so acute a comprehension of their subjects, I begin to entertain doubts. With what his friend Lord Cranbrook wrote in his introduction I certainly agree: 'These witty and observant drawings are worthy of Gilbert White's great and enduring book', and with John Lewis that 'It is indeed a splendid swansong to his work as an illustrator'[22].

It is the culmination of some forty-seven illustrated books. He mastered various media. One in which he produced some of his most impressive works was wood engraving. Among the notable qualities of his best work in all the media he used was his power of making the spectator feel that he was seeing the subject for the first time. For instance 'Common Objects', an early wood engraving of 1924, represents a cat in front of a sofa, a stool and an unseen fire: common objects indeed, yet represented – in particular the cat – in a way that makes it difficult for one's attention to be withdrawn. In *The History of Wood Engraving* Bliss thus compared John with Paul: 'He is more sensitive and whimsical, more interested in natural objects for their own sakes. Podgy old men or langourous cats are not merely shapes or forms'. Reviewing the book, John wrote, 'We hear so much about spontaneity, it is much to be desired in mediums which lend themselves to it. The brush or the pencil can be handled loosely . . . engraving demands a tight control and respectful deliberation . . . the engraver should know exactly what he is about to do within the limits of the block. Here chance and extempore decisions . . . are the last elements to depend on'[23].

In two books in particular he observed with outstanding success his own instructions, namely, *Poisonous Plants* and *Flowers and Faces*, published in 1935. The latter he himself preferred 'particularly from the point of view of precision'. The best of their illustrations, 'Thorn Apple' and 'Marrow and other Autumn Fruit and Flowers' – to name one example from each – are surely as fine as any engravings of

Below: 'Marrow and other Autumn Fruit and Flowers', wood engraving from *Flowers and Faces* by H. E. Bates (Golden Cockerel Press, 1935).

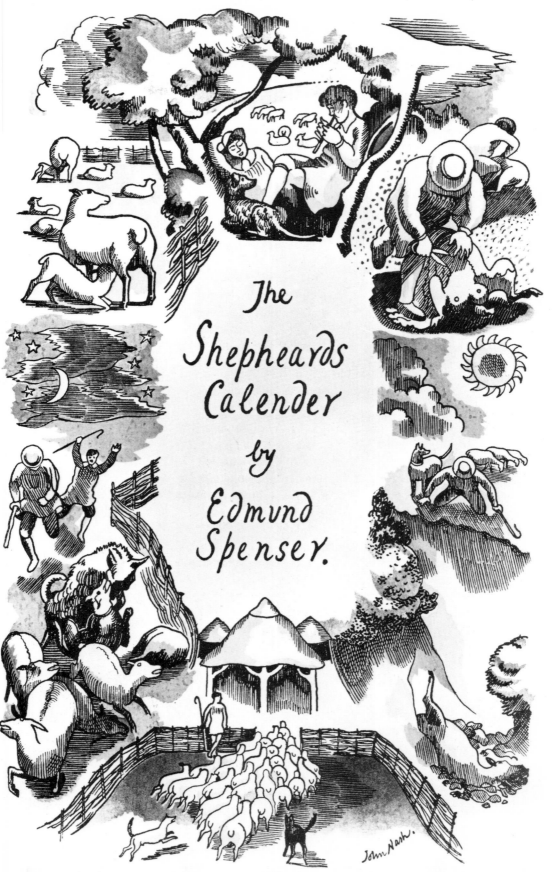

The
Shepheards
Calender
by
Edmund
Spenser.

John Nash.

our times. It is therefore strange that having so quickly and so completely mastered a difficult medium, the man able to create a work so various in its components of flowers, fruit and vegetables, yet forming so close-knit a unity, should simply have given it up.

After the completion of *Flowers and Faces* he never wielded the graver again. John Lewis, who knows more than I about John as an engraver, wrote that having mastered the medium 'he became bored with it', and this combined with the fact that private presses 'one of the main sources of commission of engravings, had nearly run their course. Also engraving on wood is a most laborious and time-taking method of illustration. . . . He could do three or four line drawings in the time it took to do one wood engraving'[24].

With all respect to the authority of Lewis, I find these explanations puzzling. John was at times haunted by the fear of poverty, but he seems to have been too dedicated an artist to abandon, without weightier cause, a technique which enabled him to produce works at once splendid and wholly different in character from his drawings. It would surely be almost impossible to tell that the title page of *The Shepheards Calender*, published in 1930, and 'Marrow and other Autumn Fruit and Flowers' from *Flowers and Faces* of five years later – to take two examples at random – were works by the same artist. Yet I cannot offer a more convincing explanation of his abandonment of wood engraving, especially as he continued to make lithographs, regarding which he said to Lewis, 'I strove nobly and long, but I never mastered the craft'[25].

He indeed did strive long, and had been encouraged in the early nineteen-twenties by the accomplished printmaker Francis Unwin, who died in 1925, after having presented John with his car. Three years later John edited 'Francis Unwin, Etcher and Draughtsman' for *The Fleuron*. John was right about his failure – a relative failure – to master the craft: his lithographs do not compare with his wood engravings or pen drawings. Yet he included four lithographs in *Wild Flowers of Britain* by his close friend Robert Gathorne-Hardy, published in 1938, and in his own *English Garden Flowers*, ten years later, there are twelve lithographs and the cover design, and several in other books as well as a large lithograph, 'The Stour at Bures' in 1937. Flowers were always an ardent preoccupation and his perceptive and skilful representations of them are innumerable.

Always, however, painting remained his most passionate preoccupation – painting, including watercolour, which although not invariably, he constantly used as its basis.

CHAPTER VII

Landscape: The Second World War

John and Christine left Gerrard's Cross in the spring of 1922 for Lane End House – in fact a large cottage – at Meadle, under the Chiltern Hills near Aylesbury, Buckinghamshire. It was the first place where they had a garden of their own, which gave scope to John's lifelong fascination with plants. From that time onwards they became one of his principal subjects, and he also kept a record of all those he grew. Lane End remained their home for the following twenty-two years. There landscape remained his most passionate preoccupation, and as Meadle is a remoter place than Gerrard's Cross he was less involved in extraneous

Meadle, Vale of Aylesbury 19¾" x 29½", oil on canvas, c.1922. This view of Meadle was probably painted shortly after John and Christine arrived there to set up their first home together. *Private Collection/Photo: Blond Fine Art*

activities and able to concentrate on it more consistently. In 1923 he made a black chalk and watercolour drawing 'The Lane' – the lane was just below their house – which was bought by the Tate the same year, the first of his works which it acquired.

However, in his work as a landscape artist at this time the crucial event was his rediscovery in 1922 of East Anglia, to which, as already mentioned, he had first been introduced ten years before by Claughton Pellew-Harvey. In 1918 he had returned briefly, travelling around and staying in Norfolk at Sheringham; here he made several paintings and drawings, both of the immediate countryside, such as the watercolour 'Landscape near Sheringham, Norfolk', and of the other places he had visited in East Anglia, such as the drawings of Wormingford Mill in Essex or the watercolour 'Cromer from the Pier', dating from 1919. After settling at Meadle he and Christine began to make a habit of travelling to other parts of the country during the summer months, returning often to places where the landscape held a particular attraction. Thus he developed a unique delight, never to diminish, in East Anglia. 'Compared with the West', he said to me, 'it's more brilliant in atmosphere, and

The Lane
Painted c.1922, this shows the view from Lane End House at Meadle. 11¼" x 15¼", black chalk and watercolour.
Trustees of the Tate Gallery, London

it's subtler, less obviously dramatic'. This delight found expression in his renting a bungalow beside Wormingford Mill on the River Stour in the summer of 1929.

The following year bungalow and Mill were both burnt down while he was there and he lost much work. In 1931 he rented the Thatched Cottage at Wiston-by-Nayland, a village on the Stour, near Bures. Here he painted regularly throughout the nineteen-thirties. The significance of this move is implicit in the fact that while neither Gerrard's Cross nor Monks Risborough, both of which he liked, were far from where he was brought up and had spent his early years, his move to East Anglia represented a radical change which he would hardly have made without a strong sense of identification with it. Several years later he finally settled there but made, in the meanwhile, a number of East Anglian landscapes in the neighbourhood of Assington, one of which, 'A Suffolk Landscape', an oil of 1936 or 1937, was bought by the Tate in 1939.

During the twenties and thirties John also travelled and painted in many other parts of the country, producing most

Avoncliffe from the Aqueduct
Oil on canvas, 33½" x 26½". This view was painted after Nash's visits to Bristol and Bath in 1925. A squared-up study for it at the Tate is dated c.1926.
Private Collection

73

notably urban and industrial views. In 1925 and 1937, on the latter occasion with Eric Ravilious, he visited Bristol, which he greatly enjoyed, especially the docks and paddle-steamers; these, he wrote, 'were the inspiration of many works'. At the same time he visited Bath, which he found equally stimulating. Of both places he made a number of watercolours and oil paintings, including, most notably, 'The Dredgers, Bristol Docks', an oil of 1925 at the Swindon Art Gallery, 'Canal Bridge, Sydney Gardens, Bath' and 'Suspension Bridge, Bath', both oils of about 1927 at the Victoria Art Gallery, Bath; also, over a decade later, 'Nocturne: Bristol Docks', a watercolour of 1938 now in the Bristol City Art Gallery. These are among the few urban views which John ever painted, in later years concentrating primarily on landscape and plant drawing. The Bristol and Bath views are comparable in subject matter to a group of paintings dating from the same period which includes 'The Viaduct', an oil of about 1928 at the Leeds Art Gallery, 'Cromer', an oil of 1929 and 'Yarmouth Docks', an oil of 1930.

Among notable landscapes besides those made in Buckinghamshire, or Essex and Suffolk are 'The Stroud Valley',

A Suffolk Landscape
Oil on Canvas, 24″ x 32″, c.1936–7. Painted near Assington, this view provides a good example of the freshness and directness of Nash's representation of nature, at times appearing to be misleadingly simple.
Trustees of the Tate Gallery, London

oil, and two of nearby Sapperton, chalk and wash, in Glou-cestershire, of 1920; 'The Walled Pond, Little Bredy, Dorset', an oil of 1923 at the Aberdeen Art Gallery and 'Farm in a Hollow' and 'The Cattle Pond, Long Bredy, Dorset', both watercolours of about 1923. There were also a few made shortly before the war in 1938 on one of his rare visits abroad, including 'Audierne, Brittany' and 'Cemetery of Boats', (also painted at Audierne), both water-colours. One place that gave him particular delight was Oxwich Bay on the Gower Peninsula, Glamorgan, where he and Christine stayed in 1939. Among the works he made there are 'Three Cliffs Bay' and 'The Beach, Llangenith', both watercolours, the latter at the Victoria and Albert Museum. It was the first of several visits to the Gower Peninsula and other parts of Wales.

There was one new activity only remotely connected with landscape painting and the cultivation or representation of

Canal Bridge, Sydney Gardens, Bath
Oil on canvas, 28″ x 30″, c.1927. Like much of Nash's work deriving from his visits to Bristol and Bath in the 1920s, this painting is based on a very balanced classical composition.
Victoria Art Gallery, Bath/ Photo: Courtauld Institute of Art, University of London

plants in which he was to become engaged over many years. He, who had never attended an art school, and usually avoided even looking at works of art other than those of his friends, became an art teacher, joining in 1924 the staff of the Ruskin School of Drawing, in not far distant Oxford, where he remained until the death, five years later, of the Master, Sidney Carline. He proved an admirable teacher and in 1934 my father, then Principal of the Royal College of Art, appointed him Assistant Teacher of Design, where, the war years apart, he remained until 1957. Here again his reputation was exceptional. He later held other similar posts, though except in one case, never teaching for more than one day a week.

For John and Christine the late nineteen-thirties were darkened by a tragedy. They had a son, born in 1930, whom they named William. One day in 1935 Christine was driving their powerful old-fashioned car, William sitting beside her, when the door on the left-hand side, which had not been securely closed, swung open and the boy began to slip out. The car was one which required both hands to control it;

Suspension Bridge, Bath
Oil on canvas, 24" x 30", c.1927. This belongs to the series of Bath views painted after Nash's visit there in 1925, and is typical of the period in its depiction of buildings and architecture as an integral part of the landscape.
Private Collection

Right, above: *Nocturne: Bristol Docks*
Watercolour, 15¾" x 23", signed and dated 1938.
Bristol City Art Gallery

Right, below: *Sand Dunes and Rocky Coast: Gower Peninsula, Glamorgan*
Pencil and watercolour, 14¼" x 21½", signed and dated 1939.
Private Collection

she held him for as long as she could, slowing to almost walking pace when suddenly she had to let go. He fell out, hit his head on the curbstone and was killed instantly. She picked him up and put his body on the back seat and drove to the hospital. There was an inquest, which John did not attend. He was devoted to the boy, whose last comics, drawing books and the like he always kept. For some years he could not bring himself to forgive Christine and the tragedy brought an element of detachment into their relations. Eventually, however, his devotion was renewed. Though frequently unfaithful, as he was indeed from shortly after their marriage, it remained – the late nineteen-thirties apart – a basically happy and constructive relationship.

When the Second World War came Nash's situation was very different from what it had been in the First. During the intervening years his reputation had greatly increased. In 1929 he was elected a member of the New English Art Club and the next year the success of his original one-man exhibition at the Goupil Gallery was followed by that of another, also at the Goupil, showing paintings, drawings, and wood engravings which were very favourably received. Similar success marked his third one-man show at the French Gallery in 1933. In the meantime, his paintings and drawings of the Western Front had made a deep impression on a number of influential men in the armed forces. In April 1939 he joined the Royal Observer Corps but the following year he was given an honorary rank of Captain in the Royal Marines for six months, as an Official Artist to the Admiralty. His attitude towards representing war subjects, however, had changed. In the First War he had made slight sketches under difficulties but derived the utmost satisfaction from painting, immediately afterwards, such works as 'Over the Top' and 'Oppy Wood'. But by the time of the Second this would no longer be the case. In a letter to the

Barnett Freedman, John Nash and Eric Ravilious photographed together in their uniforms as Official War Artists in 1940.
Collection Helen Binyon

'Interruption on the Quayside'

Curator of Works of Art at the Imperial War Museum he wrote from Meadle on 16 April 1940 '. . . now I am again an Official War Artist, this time attached to the Navy. I fear, that after 20 years, the spark of inspiration will be somewhat dulled, besides, what a War!'

He served as a War Artist at Plymouth, Bristol and Swansea. Convinced that he had already expressed his response to war in his works relating to the First World War, he applied through the Royal Marines for an active posting. As Paul wrote to Gordon Bottomley in early May 1943: 'Jack . . . is a pukka captain in the Royal Marines on a hush-hush job somewhere in Scotland at this moment. . . . He didn't like being an official artist for the Admiralty – couldn't do anything, he said and just went on nagging until he got into active service. Was there ever such a chap.'[26] On 30 March 1941 he was commissioned a temporary

'Interruption on the Quayside' Both Ravilious and Nash found the traditions of Royal Navy etiquette a little confusing to cope with as War Artists. Here, a sketch from one of Nash's letters written in 1940.
Collection Helen Binyon

Captain instead of an honorary one, served later as an Acting Temporary Major in the Royal Marines, and was ordered to Rosyth where he served as a Staff Officer and later to Portsmouth, under the Commander-in-Chief, and then under the Vice-Admiral, in Dover, where his principal duties related to the Camouflage and Deception installations along the coast from there to Portland. Eventually he was given a still more responsible undertaking at Portsmouth, where he was joined by Christine, who served in the W.V.S. canteen in the dockyard. Here in 1941 he made a detailed series of aircraft identification notes, and wrote the foreword to a no less detailed illustrated pamphlet on aircraft recognition. In November 1944 he was discharged with the rank of Temporary Captain.

His drawings – he made scarcely any paintings – as an Official Artist in the Second World War are fairly numerous, but he is represented at the Imperial War Museum by 'Two Submarines by a Jetty', 'HMS Oracle at Anchor', watercolours, 'A Dockyard Fire', an oil, and a folio of eighteen miscellaneous sketches. Seventeen additional pictures, also products of his Second World War commission, were distributed at the end of the war among various national museums throughout the Commonwealth.

Two Submarines by a Jetty Watercolour, 9¾" x 15¾", 1941. The First World War had had a far greater effect on Nash at the age of 24 then the Second had on him at the age of 47; this difference is reflected in the relative lack of immediacy and involvement in his war paintings of the 1940s. *Trustees of the Imperial War Museum, London*

80

CHAPTER VIII
The Move to Bottengoms

After John's discharge from the forces in 1944, he and Christine sold their cottage at Meadle and moved into Bottengoms Farmhouse near Wormingford, Essex, which, with some two acres of land, they had bought for £750 the previous year. It remained their home for the rest of their lives. The name 'Bottengoms' is understood to derive from Bottingham, that of a Saxon farmer. The farmhouse is a small, two-storied sixteenth or seventeenth-century building, of wood and plaster, with one brick gable-end. There are no passages inside; the three main rooms, sitting-room, kitchen and dining-room are low-ceilinged, opening one into the other. From the kitchen a small, steep staircase leads up to bedrooms and to John's studio, a small L-shaped room with two windows separated by a chimney-stack. The windows look out onto a characteristic John Nash landscape – so characteristic that one has a momentary sense of looking at one of his paintings.

When they settled there it was a primitive place. 'The source of water', wrote John Lewis, 'was from a stream that ran in an open culvert across the kitchen floor, which made the kitchen somewhat colder than the garden outside'[27]. They had some difficulty in moving in, for the van they hired was unable to carry their possessions as far

Bottengoms Farmhouse in Essex, which the Nashes bought in 1943.
Collection Ronald Blythe

as the farm because of the branches that hung low over the long, rough, narrow and winding road which leads from Wormingford. In consequence they had to unload all their possessions, including two pianos, a third of a mile from the farm. There they waited for several hours until they were able to hire a horse and cart to bring them to their new home. The move completed, Christine would then bicycle to and from Colchester and begin setting up the home, sometimes sleeping on a camp-bed in the granary.

John became attached to the Stour Valley as he had never been to any other place, a place which – according to Sickert – Gainsborough and Constable had between them left 'a sucked orange'. Even though signposts bear the names of Constable landscapes John responded to it as if it had been a discovery of his own. The zest of his response he preserved, however, as he had for the landscapes round Gerrard's Cross and Monks' Risborough, from the remotest possibility of becoming too familiar, by working elsewhere, usually in spring and summer in various places among them St Austell, Cornwall, where he painted the nearby china-clay workings. These annual working visits – which continued

Late Summer, Stoke-by-Nayland, Suffolk
Oil on canvas, 28″ x 36″, 1951. Stoke-by-Nayland, on the opposite side of the Stour Valley to Wormingford, is within easy walking distance of Bottengoms. Nash's directness of vision here was quite uninhibited by the legacy of Constable.
Bristol City Art Gallery/Photo: Royal Academy of Arts

up to the last years of his life – took him and Christine to a variety of places, staying with or accompanied by close friends. Edward Bawden often travelled with them, and in an illuminating letter of 24 April 1979 which I was fortunate to receive from him he humorously describes the way in which these summer tours were organised

> On five occasions we shared a painting expedition in Wales on the Gower Peninsula & again near Haverfordwest at Littlehaven; in Cornwall during a cold wet spell of misery in the De Lank Quarry at Blisland; at Dunwich in Suffolk & in Shropshire at Ironbridge.
>
> If the Nashes were thinking of an excursion Christine would set off alone to make a reconnaissance & it was on her report of the pictorial potential of the selected place that John acted. On arrival & having settled in John would make a desultory sally to have a look round, returning shortly in a fairly gloomy state of mind, saying little or nothing unless by happy chance he had spotted a little-known wild plant. Such a discovery induced a friendlier attitude to an alien countryside & soon he could

China Clay Matterhorn
Watercolour, 17½″ x 22″, signed and dated 1952. This view of a china-clay workings near St Austell in Cornwall illustrates Nash's interest in the more abstract aspects of landscape.
Private Collection/Photo: Fine Art Society

JoNR on the granite peaks

be seen walking around with a small sketchbook, standing now & again to draw something & as the days went by he might be seen sitting on a stool doing a more elaborate drawing.

On John's last expedition with Edward Bawden to Shropshire the party also included Carel Weight, who told me that John 'never worked feverishly, however urgent the need to complete a picture, but in a calm, easy-going way'. In a letter of September 1956 to Griselda Lewis, John described the three artists at work together.

> The Iron Bridge is very handsome but a teaser to draw with three upright supports and five curved spans to every three so that a sideways view is very complicated. . . . We dodge between the showers and somehow I've done three drawings and a bit – but Carel has done an oil painting every day it seems while Edward keeps his work secretly in his rooms and does not divulge progress. Carel and I play bar billiards every night, but Bawden will not join these simple diversions.[28]

Although it was Christine who usually went ahead to explore districts, find rooms and choose subjects, occasionally John had to choose for himself. 'Arriving in a locality', he said to me, 'I feel like a sporting dog which will smell

Sketching at the De Lank Quarries with Edward Bawden Ink and wash, 4½″ x 6¾″, undated. Bawden and Nash often shared painting expeditions together.
Private Collection/Photo: Courtauld Institute of Art, University of London

out a bird, "there is something here" and I walk about until I find the exact place'. When he joined her they went out together, he taking with him a mass of equipment and making watercolours or more often squared-up drawings to be coloured indoors. From the completed studies he considered most appropriate he would make oils, on a table in his studio at home.

From 1962 onwards they often went to Cornwall, making five or six visits in all. These were all made with Anstice Shaw, who described them to me in July 1979.

I acted as driver and spent a great deal of time creeping round Cornish lanes and waiting for John to say in his rather precise voice 'That'll do, dear – that'll do *nicely*' leaving me to manoeuvre the car into some impossible gateway or up some perpendicular slope adjoining an estuary! We circumnavigated the 'Cornish Alps' near St Austell one year until I was dizzy. Christine came too of course as she was an excellent site spotter, and they would both twitter gently to one another when a good site came in view.

Skye was another favourite place, visited almost annually from 1957 onwards. Here the Nashes stayed with Barbara

Ironbridge, Shropshire
Watercolour, 15½″ x 21¾″, c.1960. This view is probably based on sketches made in 1956 when Nash went on a sketching expedition to Shropshire with Edward Bawden and Carel Weight. *Private Collection/Photo: Royal Academy of Arts*

and John Langston at Peinmore in Portree; Barbara recalled these visits in a letter to me of May 1980.

I do not myself think that for painting Skye was John's country. Great vistas and dramatic scenery always made him uneasy. Nevertheless he did a great deal of work on all his visits and his Skye pictures sold well. The best of them, 'The Quiraing' is an oil painting made on his first visit. What John really loved was the life in Skye – fishing, picnics and expeditions and dinner parties. All our friends made a great fuss of him. And, of course, the variety and quantity of wild flowers and the long light summer nights were a constant enchantment. . . .

Earlier in the same letter Barbara says that she remembers John and Christine not so much for the visits they made to Skye, but rather in the setting of Bottengoms. '. . . my memories are mainly of quiet weeks at Bottengoms where like old friends we communicated in a sort of private short-hand of jokes and allusions quite unintelligible to others!' During the winter – John's favourite season as an artist – the energy and curiosity which led to the summer expeditions were concentrated on the countryside around the Nashes' farmhouse, where, one of his neighbours told me, John painted 'everything in the district'. It was rightly said of him that he travelled furthest when he stayed at home.

It was here that he spend the happiest, most active and socially the most enjoyable years of his life, marred sadly in the early years by Paul's death after an attack of pneumonia. 'It was Margaret who insisted I couldn't die when the specialist said I must', Paul wrote to Gordon Bottomley in early April 1946. '"You don't know him" says she, "he's a creative artist and he still has some work to do" – just like that!'[29] Some months afterwards he and Margaret visited Dorset, wishing to see the sea. On the night of 10 July 1946 he died peacefully at Christchurch, aged fifty-seven.

For John this period was exceptionally productive: he suffered little interruption and his environment was a continuing source of inspiration, in particular, as it always had been, the presence, and here it was all but omnipresence, of water, whether spring, pond, waterfall, stream or ditch. For instance, of his twelve works at the Tate four feature water, while examples of his work of the Bottengoms period which include water abound. This series ranges from 'Mill Pond, Evening', an oil of 1946 at the Laing Art Gallery, Newcastle-upon-Tyne, 'Boxted Pool, Essex' and 'Pool in the Woods', both watercolours of 1953, 'The Lake, Little Horkesley Hall, Essex', an oil of 1958 at the Royal Academy, and 'Trees by a Stream', a watercolour of 1964.

Among the outstanding examples known to me is 'Frozen Ponds', an oil of 1959, painted in his garden at Bottengoms, a complex subject presented with simple grandeur – a masterpiece.

Life at Bottengoms was very social. Though he never allowed sociability to disturb his work John formed a circle of close friends, almost all of them neighbours, 'the dear ones' as he called them. These included Robert and Natalie Bevan, Colin and Marian Benham, Cedric Morris, Lett Haines, David and Pamela Pearce, John and Griselda Lewis, Fidelity, Lady Cranbrook and Ronald Blythe. He had a few friends who were not neighbours, among these the closest were Clarence Elliott and John and Barbara Langston, who lived in The Boltons, Chelsea when not in Skye. He was also on very friendly terms with Colonel C. H. Grey and his second wife Cecily, with whom he often stayed both before and after the war. Grey's daughter Marie remembers John teaching her stepmother the techniques of flower drawing when she was engaged in illustrating her husband's three-volume book *Hardy Bulbs*, published in 1937; with her John also played piano duets, mainly Mozart, and she remembers, too, his anxious enjoyment as he struggled to keep up with her. She also recalls the botanical discussions and arguments between John and her formidable father, who had a commercial nursery garden, and

Wormingford Mill Pond, Evening
Oil on canvas, 20″ x 30″, c.1946. One of the many local views to which Nash would often return during his years at Bottengoms.
Laing Art Gallery, Newcastle/ Photo: Courtauld Institute of Art, University of London

Mill Buildings, Boxted, Essex
Oil on canvas, 28″ x 32″, 1962.
One of many views of the mill
and mill pond which Nash
painted.
*Trustees of the Tate Gallery,
London*

how much John enjoyed the wide variety of plants and discussing the catalogues. She and her husband, Sir William Hayter, bought a number of his paintings and watercolours and inherited others belonging to her father and stepmother. These included one early work dating from the days when John could not afford a large canvas, consequently joining two small ones together to produce the size he required. His circumstances were very different when they saw him years later at Bottengoms and he told them that he could sell what he wished but was anxious not to part with anything he considered below his highest standards. They met only occasionally but wrote frequently. The Hayters remember the zest with which he talked about his 'patrons' and how touched they were to be numbered among them.

At Bottengoms, now sufficiently successful to live as they liked, John and Christine adopted regular habits. In spite of his tendency to suffer from long bouts of melancholia

and constantly from arthritis, the Bottengoms years were so enjoyable largely owing to Christine's devotion: whenever possible she continued to keep from him anything likely to cause him worry, remained an excellent and elaborate cook, and continued to look after his financial affairs. When, for instance, he went to London to attend meetings at the Royal Academy – he was elected an A.R.A. in 1940 and an R.A. in 1951 – she would give him five pounds and on his return he handed her the change. His association with the Royal Academy, of which he was an extremely loyal and conscientious member, was a constant source of satisfaction to him and of amusement to Paul: 'Just the place for you', he said. He worked intensively on his quota of six oils or watercolours for the Academy's Summer Exhibition, only returning to work in his garden after Sending-in Day.

John and Christine evolved a way of life which was perfectly suited to them both. Christine would get up at about seven, a tall, elegant figure, wearing, when the season

Frozen Ponds
Oil on canvas, 23″ x 29″, 1959. One of Nash's outstanding Winter scenes, painted at the bottom of his garden at Bottengoms.
Private Collection

allowed, a rose in her hair, and would have tea with her cat beside their coke stove. She also prepared and served in their bedroom, tea for any guests who might be staying and made a flask for the postman, who had to come down their long and awkward drive. John would appear some two hours later, carefully dressed, wearing a cravat or a tie, and they breakfasted together in the pleasant kitchen, between the drawing-room and dining-room, a place she particularly liked as it enabled her to maintain, while she cooked, communication with visiting friends. Their breakfast was substantial, including home-made bread. John began work about ten, in the studio overlooking the Stour valley, eating, by way of lunch, odds and ends by himself. At about four, they would have a substantial tea together, to which friends were often invited, served on two tables – including scones made after lunch – in front, when it was cold or cool, of a big fire. After tea he rarely worked. At six they had drinks, he whisky, though never much, and she sherry. While she cooked elaborate dinners, 'spoiling' him, he sometimes played the piano for an hour or so, or else they played duets, then listened to the radio, watched television, he enjoying sport and such performances as Cops and Robbers programmes. If these proved specially amusing they dined late, at about nine. If they had no social engagements they sat beneath a lamp, she sewing, he writing letters, for he liked to be in frequent communication with his friends. They also read widely. Fortunately he was on friendly terms with Ernest Rhys, the editor of Everyman's Library and thus had access to many classics, taking special pleasure in Jane Austen, Richardson and Smollett. He also particularly enjoyed biographies of generals and detective stories, as well as books on gardening, of which he had collected a great number, and fishing. Among his favourite works were Gilbert White's *The Natural History of Selborne* and George Borrow's *The Bible in Spain* (a copy of which he carried in his breast pocket while on active service, by way of protecting his heart); also George Nicholson's *Dictionary of Gardening* (1887), Wilfrid Blunt's *The Art of Botanical Illustration* and Mozart's *Letters*. Of books on art and artists there were relatively few.

John often invited a friend to be with them. Dreading being alone, when Christine was away he would call for Ronald Blythe, author of *Akenfield* and other books, whom he thought of as a son, and who always spent Christmas with them. He enjoyed evening parties in the neighbourhood with their friends, especially 'the dear ones'. These friends and several others often stayed with the Nashes; the Nashes stayed also with them. Christine cared less than he for social occasions, preferring public activities, such as the W.V.S.; she was an able actress and used to organise amateur dramatics.

The interior of the house offered a startling contrast to their elegant way of dressing in the evening, their luxurious dinners and the stylish tenor of their lives. Pictures destined for or returned from exhibitions leaned against furniture and walls. Books and papers – including correspondence that in any other household would have been discreetly locked away – were scattered everywhere it being understood that neither would read the other's. There were also many ashtrays, both being such heavy smokers that the dull cream walls and the ceilings were steadily darkened, but there were also many vases of flowers.

Among their intimate friends were a married couple who afforded them invaluable help: Robert Bevan, son of his old friend Robert Polhill Bevan, a leading member of the Camden Town Group, and Natalie, formerly married to Lance Sieveking, who lived at nearby Boxted House. Bevan was the chairman of S. H. Benson. It was he who proposed that John undertake one of his most amusing illustrated books, *Happy New Lear*, published in 1959 by Guinness.

Natalie Bevan had known John almost all her life, and was an exceptionally close friend even among his circle of intimates and looked after him during his periodic spells of ill-health. She kindly gave me some of her impressions of him:

John was a dressy little man. On his last visit to my cottage in Aldeburgh, a few months before he died, he insisted upon going to the hairdresser's, where they snipped the little fringe round the back of his head and charged him 15/-. 'Do I look all right, dear?' he said, giving a sweep with his hands to his hair. Then we crossed the road to the smartest man's shop in Aldeburgh, and bought two expensive cravats. 'One for you, dear', he said. When I pointed out that it was not my colour he seemed delighted to have them both.

He loved driving and even when he was crippled with arthritis, he said he felt absolutely at ease and somehow free from all constriction and in complete command of the car. He had an absolutely perilous steep winding car-rutted drive of about a mile down to his house, along which he manoeuvred magnificently.

He relied tremendously on Christine – 'Help me dear', in this and that all the time. He did not like it at all when she was not there to advise, suggest and make him happy and comfortable in every way. Christine was a wonder.

John was a great grumbler – in the nicest sort of way but he was always at it. The light – the quality of the canvas – sometimes the food – politics – friends. Bobby was always teasing him. 'Go on, John, stop grumbling' or 'Stop it, John, do stop grumbling'.

He really loved a good tea, with lots of different jams and cakes made by Christine, and other delicacies brought in by friends.

It was an utter pleasure to go for a walk with John – everything came to life and looked quite different and more interesting through his eyes. Even fishing was a pleasure; sitting beside him and listening to him talking about the landscape and the sky, and all the different lights and shades and shadows.

Although John sold almost everything he painted or drew that he thought worth selling, he and Christine felt themselves, sometimes to an almost pathological degree, hard up. This led them to be careful over spending, though never mean – careful except when their seasonal working travel

The Barn, Wormingford
Oil on canvas, 26″ x 32½″, 1954. This was Nash's Diploma work presented to the Royal Academy after his election as an Academician in 1951.
Royal Academy of Arts

was concerned, when they inclined to extravagance. Bevan persuaded him to ask higher prices for his work and obtained for him several well-paid commissions.

Other very close friends were Lord and Lady Cranbrook whom John came to know through the Sievekings, when Natalie Bevan was married to Lance Sieveking. In the early nineteen-thirties they used to see a lot of John and Christine and occasionally Paul, but after the tragic death of the Nashes' son William they saw little of them as John found it painful to be with parents surrounded by their children – two sons and three daughters. After the war they met again, and from 1947 onwards the Nashes would stay with the Dowager Lady Cranbrook during the Aldeburgh Festival. The Cranbrooks would often help John in exhibiting during the Festival – in 1947 he contributed to an exhibition of the work of East Anglian artists, also serving on the selection committee, and in 1950 he illustrated the programme with drawings of plants and local landscapes. The friendship between the Nashes and the Cranbrooks soon became deep and enduring, and John collaborated with Lord Cranbrook illustrating books – *The Natural History of Selborne*, as mentioned earlier, and *Parnassian Molehill*, an anthology of Suffolk verse written between 1327 and 1864, edited by Lord Cranbrook, and published in 1953.

The two also shared a delight in fishing, which they pursued almost to the end of their lives. During the first Aldeburgh Festival, Lord Cranbrook, in the garden of Great Glemham House, gave John instructions on how to cast a dry fly, and when John and Christine stayed with them at Banks, their sheep farm in Westmorland, he caught his first trout in a nearby pond. It was an exciting occasion, for he had hitherto been only a coarse fisherman. Once initiated, as Lord Cranbrook said, 'he took off'. Conversant with fly-fishing, he used his rod not only in local lakes and rivers but in remote places such as Skye. Lady Cranbrook recalls the last occasion when they fished together. 'I had gone to fetch them home from a reservoir near Bottengoms', she wrote, 'and found them, for once, ready to come home, because Jock [her husband] was so blind with cataract and John so fumble-fingered with arthritis neither of them had been able to tie the casts! This caused them great merriment and I found them in fits of laughter – at intervals bursting into some Harry Lauder song!!'

In spite of John being very much a country gentleman in habits and manner of dressing, and having a deeply conservative traditional outlook, he had a positive, indeed an extreme, dislike of Christianity. For this attitude none of the friends to whom I have spoken can account. There was

John Nash with the Earl of
Cranbrook fishing on the River
Stour at Wiston in 1958.
Photo: Kurt Hutton

nothing saccharine about his talk; he could be quite sharp-
tongued, yet he was a man of outstanding charm. One
friend said to me, 'He was not a moralizer, but extremely
courteous'; and yet another, 'He was out of date in his
voice and even more in his ideas'. Odd characteristics for a
man who, in his youth at least, was regarded as something
of a revolutionary.

   With the years his health declined, he suffered increasingly from melancholia, arthritis, hernia (which compelled
him to wear a truss) and frequently from influenza. It was
perhaps his health that made him, if a devoted (in spite
of his frequent infidelities) also an extremely demanding
husband. Devoted as Christine was she needed some respite,
and in order to have some time alone went shopping on

every weekday. This John couldn't understand: 'I once offered the old girl £30 if she would stock up', he said. He was, wrote John Lewis, 'a monumental grumbler . . . and oblivious of any discomfort he might cause his friends or his wife by his demands'.

Yet few men had more devoted or more loyal friends, both among his neighbours and his fellow artists. No artist, at least of his generation, took less part in London art politics, in spite of his close attachment to the Royal Academy. In Essex it was conspicuously otherwise. Together with his friends and neighbours Sir Cedric Morris, (unlike John an extremely cosmopolitan artist) and Lett Haines, who shared a house at Hadleigh, John was a founder of the Colchester Art Society and its chairman, subsequently its president. Under his influence exhibitions were held of the work of both professional and amateur artists; to these shows he regularly sent his own work. A friend told me that he never showed a hint of superiority in spite of his outstanding reputation.

Pen and ink drawing for *The Art of Angling* by Trevor Housby (Evans, 1965). *Photo: Blond Fine Art*

CHAPTER IX

Plantsman and Teacher of Plant Illustration

When he lived at Lane End House John began keeping a growing collection of gardening catalogues in the earth closet at the end of his garden, where they came in for constant study. At Bottengoms he created an unforgettably romantic garden, in which ordinary plants grew side by side with exotics. He delighted in the contrasts between their names, for instance *Dad's Favourite* and *Cappadocian Venus's Navel*. The plants were grown in beds of no particular design, but were themselves of astonishing variety. He grew plants, but did not design a garden, an art of a different order of creativity. How impassioned a gardener he was is clear from a sentence in an undated letter to Edward Bawden: 'For years I have tried, not without some success, to be both a professional painter *and* an amateur gardener. One day I expect one of the roles will give way and I assure you it will be (regretfully) the gardener'. In *The Artist Plantsman*[30], he describes the most crucial event that began his dual career as a gardener and a student of plants, and his representation of them; in short, as an 'artist plantsman':

From [the] Six Hills nursery I ordered an Alpine Plant notoriously difficult to grow. The plant belied the name on the label and some miserable usurper appeared. I complained and received apologies with a replacement. Impressed by this courtesy, I sent the manager a small wood engraving of a Bee Orchis. This was the beginning of a long friendship with the Nurseryman, Plant Collector, or, as he preferred it, 'Gardener', Clarence Elliott, and was an introduction to a vastly extended world of horticulture, where Elliott knew everyone. I used to draw the plants he had collected on his expeditions to the Andes and the Falkland Islands and elsewhere, not excluding finds in English gardens, which he maintained were the best hunting-ground. . . .

'Foxglove' from *Poisonous Plants* (Etchells & Macdonald, 1927).

Clarence Elliott was in fact the most learned of the various authorities who stimulated and broadened his knowledge of plants. He was also one of the few of John's close friends who was not a neighbour – he lived at Broadwell, Moreton-in-the-Marsh, Gloucestershire – and they carried on a lively correspondence. Writing to Edward Bawden on 25 October 1956, John described a fishing expedition with Elliott: we 'only caught a fish apiece but it was very enjoyable, not least observing the energy of a man of 76 who had two serious cancer operations yet fished a mile and a half of river on a hot day for 4 hours on end and after a short nap on returning settled down at 11.30 pm to write his weekly article on Gardening for the Ill[ustrated] London News and returned to bed at 2 am – his usual hour!' Another influence on John was 'Jason Hill', the pseudonym for Anthony Hampton, author of *The Curious Gardener*, published in 1932 and featuring five full-page line-drawings by John.

John himself began to write about gardening, contributing articles to *Gardening Illustrated* and being assigned to cover speciality sections of the Chelsea Flower Show, such as the Alpine or Herbaceous Plants, or the 'New and Rare Plants' section:

> This particular tent had an almost holy atmosphere about it. One tiptoed in with feelings of high expectancy. Very few other people were there, the big marquees flaunting their best displays, drew off all but the dedicated plantsmen. Here were plants straight from outlandish habitats, the fruits of the intrepid collector. Here also were the new 'cultivars' [a term then unused] painfully reared over long periods by single-minded horticulturalists.

Logically, John soon started illustrating books about plants, fulfilling his role as 'artist plantsman'. His first commission was sponsored by Clarence Elliott: a Six Hills Nursery catalogue, which probably cost the Nursery a substantial sum. This was followed the next year (1927) by *Poisonous Plants*, for which, as mentioned earlier, John also wrote the introduction. The next major work came eleven years later: *Plants with Personalities*. He wrote that this 'was one of the books I particularly enjoyed illustrating. The subjects were dictated and specimens mostly sent to me to draw – a very hazardous business – *Tibouchina semi-decandra* was sent three times in ladies' stays boxes before a reasonable specimen sustained the post'. In following years he continued to illustrate botanical projects, often collaborating in the choice of plants:

'Shingle Plants' from *The Curious Gardener* by Jason Hill (Faber & Faber, 1932).

In *English Garden Flowers* (1948) the choice of subjects was my own, as well as the written parts. *The Tranquil Gardener* (1958) and *The Native Garden* (1961) by Robert Gathorne-Hardy benefited from the close and understanding collaboration which long friendship and conformity of tastes produce. *The Curious Gardener*, *The Contemplative Gardener* and *The Tranquil Gardener*, their moods follow on very properly, and the artist should be content to accompany them. Further titles on these lines would be hard to invent – tranquillity has the last word.

After settling at Bottengoms John began teaching plant illustration at the Flatford Mill Field Centre, which he also describes:

This started chiefly with the ideal of drawing the British Flora, but a visit to a local garden full of rare bulbs and herbaceous 'exotica' led to defections from the original purpose. There was no wish to spurn the humble forms of our native flora, but they stood a poor chance against the riches of colour and the wealth of form provided by the garden exotics. We wanted to draw our plants with

'Aeonium Holochrysum with
Kleinia Neriifolia and
Aporocactus Flagelliformis'.
This pen and ink drawing of
Robert Gathorne-Hardy's
conservatory appeared in his
book, *The Tranquil Gardener*,
(Nelson, 1958).
Photo: Anthony d'Offay

some freedom, giving them air and light and even decorative values, but at the same time to conform to the title of our course. The distinction between a good and a bad plant drawing is hard to make. If you look at the plant-draughtsman's Bible, Wilfrid Blunt's *Botanical Illustration*, you will find some illustrations which conform to the need for accuracy combined with the spark of a live drawing, as well as much work which may serve its purpose but gives no feeling of the living subject.

For nearly seventy years I have drawn plants for love or necessity and have never destroyed even slight sketches or notes in case they should be needed for reference (publishers can have an awkward habit of asking for illustrations in the 'dead' season). In any case, I feel a slight pencil flourish even of part of a plant is more valuable than a photograph. The open innocent countenance of a

Eomecon Chionantha
Pencil and watercolour, 13¾"
x 9¾", signed and dated 1930.
Photo: Anthony d'Offay

Stems U.y Gr. red-m points — leaves above dull y.gr. glaucous under
lower leaves brighter y.gr.y.gr.
Eomecon chionantha
Meadle Aug. 1930

John Nash

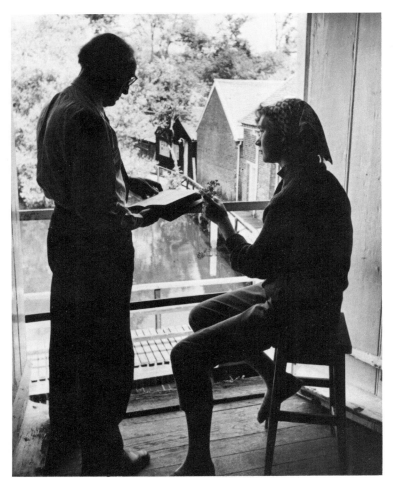

John Nash with Jennifer
Andrews at the Flatford Mill
Field Study Centre.
Photo: Kurt Hutton

Daisy or Anemone may seem easy to draw, but they too
can prove to be a snare, and sometimes I prefer the
hooded Labiates, helmeted Monkshood and Balsam, or
the leering countenance of Foxglove and Pentstemon.

John Lewis has dealt with John's drawings, wood engravings and writings on plants, but here this extract quoted
from John's own *Artist Plantsman*, which gives so lucid
and succinct a description of the botanical aspect of his art
will suffice. For his depiction of plants is in essence so close
to that of landscape, so direct, so wholly concentrated on
the subject, so precisely informed, that there is no radical
difference between them, other than those of subject and
technique. Jennifer Andrews was one of his students at the
Flatford Mill Field Centre, first attending there in 1959,
and becoming one of John's close friends. She had an intense
passion for plants and understood fully John's approach to
drawing them. There follows her account of her experience
of John's teaching at Constable's spectacularly beautiful
house where he gave a week's course yearly:

'Rosa Variegata de Bologna,
Reine des Violettes and Nuits
de Young' from *The Tranquil
Gardener*.
Photo: Royal Academy of Arts

As well as the actual words that were spoken, it was the
atmosphere surrounding John's courses at Flatford Mill
which made the week so stimulating and rewarding –
unique. He brought with him an aura, a presence,
commanding respect. And you felt that he respected your
work, but he could be outspoken. 'Whatever is this?' at
a rather feeble daub of colour in a landscape. Then he
would find something to praise, making you feel better!

He communicated a sense of wonder at growing things
– 'See how that leaf *tucks in* under the flower' – You felt
that he was amazed also, spurred on to give of your best
and more. His very presence seemed to set a standard of
work with no limits.

John had a captivating way of guiding you along –
'You might like to add "Mermaid" to your collection of
roses'. There was no question of not doing so.

He did not spend a great amount of time looking over
your shoulder. An hour might pass with him poring over

Himalayan Blue Poppy
Pencil drawing. 14″ x 9¼″,
signed and dated June 1928.
Photo: New Grafton Gallery

books to find the correct Latin name for each flower that was being drawn. These would be written painstakingly on the blackboard, to be added to the bottom of your work. Or, seeing us all absorbed, he would go quietly out and soon be seen beside the mill-pond, fishing rod in hand although he once wrote to me 'I don't think there *are* any fish in that mill pool'. Later he would be back. 'Dear – I'm so sorry, I haven't taken any notice of you all day'. And his whole attention would be on your problems, quietly suggesting, every suggestion memorable.

'Bring the stem to its logical conclusion'. Sometimes he would make a comment just as you were starting, which would immediately put you on the right lines.

Always John's modesty was apparent – 'I don't attempt anything like you girls'. At times he seemed almost diffident about giving practical advice, but he passed on to me one absolutely invaluable colour recipe.

His sense of fun – 'What's this, a free-for-all?' at my crowded page of flowers. And at Bottengoms he would say 'Look out!' and make the hard black seeds of Himalayan Balsam jump at you, for your delight – and for his own!

At the weekend, John would come into the studio to say 'I'm going home now'. He put on a scowl. 'And mind you are all working when I get back.'

The aim of these courses was to make accurate drawings with artistic liveliness. Somebody once produced a pair of calipers. I heard John's voice behind me saying 'Hand and eye only here'. The calipers were not seen again.

The Warden – a botanist – was once critical of the fact that I had drawn a group of flowers too large. John snorted his disapproval of the criticism. He liked the piece of work and said it should remain as it was. He once told me 'I sometimes draw too small, to my annoyance'.

Once, approving of one of my drawings he made a gesture over it with his stiff hand. He must have spoken, but I cannot recall the exact words. The gesture is one of my happiest memories. He was delighted at his popularity

Cottage Window Plants
Lithograph, 30″ x 19½″, 1945. This was one of two lithographs Nash did for a company called Contemporary Lithographs, which John Piper and Robert Wellington set up to organize the making and marketing of prints for schools. The signature was added later for a friend.
Private Collection

and sales at a late age 'after all these years. But what use is money?' He stumped angrily away. The arthritis was telling. This was the only time I heard him speak bitterly.

Again with delight – 'Here I sit [in his own studio] like a spider in my den and they all come to me'.

I was a daily student on John's last course, and as I was not fond of working by electric light, I tended not to stay after dinner. But because John was there, one evening I made a point of doing so. Soon he came into the studio, and within moments there was a burst of merriment. I turned in my seat, looking through the jungle of flowers we had collected to see John in the centre of a group of students. Everyone was laughing. That is how I like to remember him, happily surrounded by people and plants.

Always hospitable, John often asked students to Bottengoms during the weekends. Jennifer Andrews often went, and she wrote: 'The beauty of his own plants was a source of constant amazement to him. We used to pick them and take them to Flatford Mill to draw. Christine was very gay and welcoming; she had trouble with her eyes and wore an eyeshade, but we didn't see her often: she was apt to be away choosing sites for him to draw and paint'.

One of John's qualities which impressed Jennifer on these visits was his rare considerateness. Everyone who worked for him was given tea – green tea – and 'made a fuss of'; and any visitor was liable to be asked to drive home the gardener and the others.

Jennifer Andrews, whose delight in portraying plants was disciplined and enhanced by the teaching of Arnold Machin and John Nash, has become an exceptionally able practitioner. What artists write does not necessarily reflect the character of their work but a few lines in the opening paragraph of an article does reflect hers.

Let us toss away once and for all the idea that flowers are purely pretty things to be arranged on paper in stiff attitudes and forced designs, as dead as stuffed birds or as foolish as circus animals. Flowers are as living and growing as we who attempt to catch their essence. They *can* be pretty, they are also wild, vital, fierce, breathtaking, dramatic – the drama of a just open stamen, fiery gold against pale petal, of blue light stabbing through purple anemone, of dark blue falling across white flower, hair case poised on a poppy bud, of hogweed bent in torment, caught in the clutches of giant bindweed. . . .[31]

Of this John would have warmly approved, I think.

CHAPTER X
Final Recognition

In spite of his lack of ambition, the increasing admiration evoked by his work (as well, I suspect, by his engaging personality) brought John increasing recognition. In 1964 the C.B.E. was conferred on him, and three years later he received an Honorary Doctorate from the University of Essex. An active member of the Committee of Management of the Minories in Colchester, he was responsible for the appointment of the first three curators and was frequently called upon to advise successive chairmen, particularly Robert Bevan.

Another sign of the increasing recognition of his work were the retrospective exhibitions held in his later years. The first of these was held in 1954 at the Leicester Galleries, affording him much pleasure. But there was one which moved him deeply: in 1967 the Royal Academy accorded him a unique tribute: a retrospective exhibition of his work featuring 263 oils, watercolours, pen-and-ink drawings and illustrated books. It was the first in its series of works by living members to be held in the Main Gallery. John devoted several months to its selection and hanging.

The exhibition was received by the press with admiration and an exceptional degree of understanding. In response to a congratulatory letter from John Lewis he showed that this afforded him immense although not unqualified satisfaction: 'I *should* be happy at the result and cannot complain on the score of Press notices but one is so contrary and the fact is I am feeling dreadfully flat now that it is launched and long to be able to start work again without quite knowing where or what. It's most unsettling and has forced my mind back to the Past without taking any account for the Future. With all that work at the R.A. it might be said "You've really done enough old sod, why not take a rest?" But I hate entire rest – besides it's not economically feasible'.[32]

John Nash in his studio. The painting on the easel is *A Breconshire Landscape. Collection Ronald Blythe*

The Royal Academy exhibition was immediately followed, by another at the Minories, Colchester sponsored by the Victor Batte-Lay Trust and the Colchester Art Society in collaboration with the Royal Academy. It was enthusaistically received: the artist was a local man, much loved and respected, and his work evoked genuine admiration. The review in the local paper, *The Colchester Express*, contained this simple yet pertinent tribute.

A painting by John Nash is like a sentence spoken by a gentleman, perfectly enunciated, quiet, complete, yet with a certain reserve about it as of things left unsaid.

Ipswich Docks
Oil on canvas, 20″ x 30″.
Painted around about 1950,
this sort of subject became
increasingly rare in Nash's later
work.
*Private Collection/Photo: New
Grafton Gallery*

The exhibition was also the occasion for an open letter to John from Edward Bawden, printed in the catalogue. Bawden was one of John's oldest friends, and in his letter he writes of their first meeting at the Royal College of Art in 1934, their shared interests in flowers and gardening, their summer painting expeditions and their visits to one another's homes. The description of Bawden's first stay with the Nashes at Monks' Risborough richly evokes the simple pleasure they derived from each other's company:

Christine and the cats stayed indoors; she was curled up sewing and each of the cats sat on a chair. Talk drifted to painting and narrowed down to the importance of tone values and soon I found you were asking questions I could not answer. It was a dilemma you resolved by tentatively suggesting the answers yourself and it must have been hard work for you to have kept the conversation going. Christine remained silent, but as the evening light faded there was a flint reflected from her glasses whenever she looked up. Now and again a cat became restive and went to have a look outside. At last when our conversation had almost died down the oil lamp was lit, the sudden brightness brought relief and Christine turned the talk into something much livelier. We all relaxed and chatted and laughed till it was time to ask about a hot-water-bottle, the position of the upstairs lavatory and whether a cup of tea would be nice in the morning.

John was very touched by this open letter, and wrote to Edward Bawden on 5 November thanking him: 'Your personal letter addressed to me in the Minories Catalogue was a pleasant surprise as I believe it was intended to be and though not arriving in the post I feel it demands a reply in writing. . . . I greatly appreciate the recalling of pleasant memories in it, not unmixed with some lighter barbs of your wit which I have taken with my usual stoicism . . .'.

In these years John was just as active as he had ever been, continuing in his pursuit of the interests he had developed since his youth. His activities were as varied as they were intensively pursued: besides being a member of the governing bodies of the Minories and the Colchester Art Society he continued as an art teacher who imbued his students with enthusiasm, a pianist, gardener, a regular fisher of pike in winter, carp and perch in summer, and he was the most social of men. During the winter he and Christine would be quite happy to venture out in the worst weather if there was the prospect of a party; it would have taken more than a snowfall to have kept him away from a party, an attitude of life of the 1920s that never left him. In January 1969 he wrote to Griselda Lewis how they were snowed in 'and had to be fetched and carried like a couple of old parcels to 2 parties'[33]. Earlier, just after Christmas 1966, he had written of his junketing to Edward Bawden:

Revolt
This printed Christmas card was one of many sent out by the Nashes over the years. Particularly close friends had theirs hand-coloured.
Private Collection

We were thinking of you spending a quiet withdrawn Xmas in London while we rushed madly from party to party in varying degrees of doubtful motoring weather. Nor was this junketing without its hazards. On Xmas Day evening we left a party at midnight in bitter cold frosty conditions & found a puncture – fortunately we were overtaken by friends leaving the party. . . . Drove us home & next day got all repaired for our next assignment. . . .

Yet in spite of his pursuit of these diverse activities John continued to paint with undiminished dedication, draw from nature, and to illustrate and contribute illustrations to many books as consistently as many artists who do little or even nothing else.

However, at this time he began to suffer increasingly from depression, aggravated by his arthritis and the resulting restrictions on his activities. In a letter to Edward Bawden of 9 March 1965 he wrote 'I have at last breasted the waves

of doubt & entered the harbour of quiet decision. I will not say that the vessel is entirely becalmed or tied up to quay-side. . . . Yes, my God, I feel like an old horse rasped by the rowell if that's the word!' However he was not nearly as philosophical in his letters to Janet Stone, who with her husband Reynolds had been a close friend over many years. His letters to her are in parts lugubrious to the point of seeming very self-indulgent; as early as the late nineteen-fifties he was writing 'Quite a number of my fellow members at the R.A. [banquet] looked tolerably blooming in their 70s, 75s etc but some are tottering on their perches & on the whole seem rather a depressing sight as a group to which I am fast adhering . . .'. What particularly depressed John was the forced inactivity which old age brought with it, as another letter to Janet of 4 May 1960 shows.

. . . This brings me to my chief moan which is that directly I had finished at the R.A. I got neuritis in my right shoulder & arm & have been idle for the last 3 weeks. Dr. told me I was exhausted & run down & the neuritis was the result. No Artwork, Fishing, Gardening or piano – just sit about & read – he said. Can you imagine how irksome this has been for me but I expect you can. . . . But I went to the [R.A.] Banquet & found myself put next to K. Clark. Arthritis & the ambiguity of our former relationship made me rather ungracious at first but I was given no time to sulk as he immediately claimed the mutual friends (Stones of course!), turned on the charm before we had opened up our napkins! . . .

In the autumn of 1976 a tragic event transformed the regular pattern of his life. A highly successful exhibition of his watercolours was held at the Buxton Mill Gallery, Buxton Lamas, Norfolk. There was a private view on a Friday evening. A gathering of many enthusiastic friends evoked the sociability to which John invariably, and Christine sometimes, responded; this occasion delighted them both and it continued until the following morning. Christine was in the highest spirits and seemed well, but a few weeks later she was dead.

During the months which followed John was looked after by Ronald Blythe, who had met the Nashes about thirty years before when he was a young poet in his early twenties. 'They were both very attracted to young people and, I should say, very attractive *to* them. For me they had an enchanting quality.' Ronald Blythe was a very close friend, becoming a writer under the prompting of the Nashes, and dedicating his first novel to Christine and *Akenfield* to John; he also made a BBC 2 film about him. 'We all three loved each other very dearly. One of the reasons was that we loved language, the voice, words on the page, etc. It was a very eloquent friendship.' In a letter of 20 May 1980 from Bottengoms, Ronald gave me the following account of the events which followed Christine's death:

I heard of Christine's death a few minutes after it occurred and immediately telephoned John asking him if I should come at once. He had friends with him and told me to come the following morning, which I did. Except for leaving him with Natalie Bevan for a few days after Christine's funeral, so that I could shut up my house I stayed with him until he too died ten months later. At first he was more amazed than grief-stricken by her death. It had great unreality for him. They had been married for 58 years and both he and all their friends accepted that 'he would go first'. It was typical of her that she died with the absolute minimum of fuss and bother.

I had stayed with him so many times in the past when she was away and was so familiar with his routine (he was something of a ritualist who liked certain little patterns made throughout the day) that he was very at ease with me. We had been friends for some thirty years, but he continued to see me as a very young man and his attitude towards me was both fatherly and dependent. He was very ill both with bad arthritis and from what was possibly a stroke suffered soon after Christine's funeral. Everything was made much worse by the death, a fortnight or so after his wife's, of his great friend John Langston. J.N. spent Christmas in bed and his sister Barbara and myself sat together downstairs.

In the New Year, John, who had great powers of recovery, but who was still obviously very ill, managed to come downstairs and even to take little walks in the garden. He watched sport on television and read a lot. I was sleeping near him in Christine's adjoining room in order to nurse him and before we dozed off we each read Jane Austen – all her novels – reading aloud some of the funny bits. He also listened to a lot of concerts on the wireless and he told me about Mozart, Schubert and other composers (he had a great knowledge of music).

A great number of people came to see him – exhausting us both! But the person who helped us most and who really made it possible for us both to go on living here – as I don't drive – was Penelope Hall, a young neighbour who did all our shopping and, indeed, anything and everything she could to assist us.

At first the district nurse came to see John about once a week. Eventually he allowed me both to bath and dress him. In February he struggled into the studio, which had been kept heated, and declared that he was going to paint. The painting was a watercolour of Skye and it was his last picture. In May he was so much better that plans were made for him to travel by car to Cornwall with Anstice Shaw, staying with the Reynolds Stones en route, but the death of Anstice's father (87) prevented his little holiday. John collapsed soon after this and I was told by his doctor that he would soon die. He became unconscious and was taken to St Mary's Hospital in Colchester, myself travelling with him in the ambulance. He eventually died in September [the 23rd, 1977]. A few hours before I was sitting with him and saw him painting or sketching in the air. He knew me and said my name.

John was buried beside Christine in Wormingford Churchyard. They had been cremated and Ronald Blythe buried their ashes in two caskets in the presence of three or four close friends and read poems by Thomas Hardy and Andrew Young.

Self Portrait
Oil on board, 16″ x 12½″.
This was probably painted in
1945.

*Private Collection/Photo: New
Grafton Gallery*

CHAPTER XI
Conclusion:
The Artist and his Aims

Perhaps the most striking characteristics of John Nash's artistic output are its individuality and its consistency throughout a long career. Several writers, including Frederick Gore in his admirable introduction to the catalogue of John's 1967 retrospective exhibition at the Royal Academy, have suggested that he was affected by a number of post-Cézanne French painters, especially by Friez, Lhote, Marchand and Marquet, in whom Percy Moore Turner, the picture dealer and friendly neighbour near Gerrard's Cross, evoked his interest. With all respect to Gore I venture to think that such interest was transitory and superficial. That they provoked his interest I do not doubt, but I am also sure that they had a no more radical effect on his work than that of the celebrated figures who became well known in London as a result of Fry's two Post-Impressionist exhibitions or even than his far more intimate knowledge of the work which he so greatly admired of Gore, Bevan, Ginner, and Gilman.

I think it is likely that his early association with the Camden Town Group served at least to confirm his own instinctive conviction that everyday subjects, represented with the utmost insight, would evoke his own best qualities. Sickert's dictum that 'the plastic arts are gross arts dealing joyfully with gross material facts'[34] is an overstatement in relation to the practice of his friends and associates of the Camden Town Group. There are few if any 'gross material facts' in the work of Gore, Bevan, Ginner, Gilman or their colleagues, but it is a clear indication, however exaggerated, of their consistent practice of representing the subjects – subjects, even if carefully selected – without a shadow of idealisation or conformity to any conventional style. Their

subjects, including Sickert's, are predominantly urban. John Nash's with relatively few exceptions, are of the British countryside, and he never felt himself to be part of any current artistic movement which would come between him and the landscape which inspired him. Of his exhibiting with the Cumberland Market Group he had written to Carrington 'How queer my little watercolours will look besides their oils'; earlier in 1914, he had written to her from Cheltenham:

> The farmyards here are so good. I think I shall do farmyard scenes for the rest of my 'natural'. I am convinced now even more than formerly that a strict adherence to nature is the only thing worth doing, even at the risk of being dull? . . . But how can nature be dull. What is cubism or anything else to nature. . . .

From his first moments as an artist John was deeply and directly moved by nature, and his early correspondence with Carrington provides an interesting background to his first paintings. In 1915 he wrote from Iver Heath:

The Farm
Oil on canvas, 17½″ x 23½″, c.1925. Painted at Meadle while the Nashes were living at Lane End House, this painting represents the sort of subject which John was to remain interested in for the rest of his life.
Private Collection/Photo: New Grafton Gallery

... I had a most marvellous walk from Clifton Hampden. On the way I saw the potato digger at work & also a motor plough, but as I came up round the back of the Wittenham Clumps a fine light burst on my gaze. A terrific purple Prussian blue storm cloud in layers covered the sky opposite the sun; against this the two clumps shot up crowned by their woods of beach of a brilliant gold orange in the sun. In the foreground were green wild rose bushes growing from a pollard stump whose leaves had turned a fine claret red. These colours against the sky produced an effect which at once arrested one's admiration and wonder. To add to this a rainbow appeared also; not to mention lesser items such as a hawk hovering bright against the same background. I stood for some time wondering at these 'natural phenomena'. Certainly Berkshire has more fascination for me than any other county. I had a long talk w. the engine driver engaged in steam ploughing & drew the engine. It is a splendid sight & gives a great idea of power. . . .

The vision of John Nash from his earliest years as a painter was too definite to allow him to be susceptible to the influence of the work of other artists however much he might admire them. His work was of course far from being literal realism – the realism that could be expressed by photographs – it was one of a kind lucidly defined by his friend Ginner in the opening sentence of his essay 'Neo-Realism'. 'All great painters', he wrote, 'by direct intercourse with Nature have extracted from her facts which others have not observed before, and interpreted them by methods which are personal and expressive of themselves – this is the great tradition of Realism'[35].

In the same article an opinion is also expressed which – although it is not applicable to the work of every painter – surely is to that of John. 'Of whatever interest a sketch may be as expressing a fleeting note, a mood, an *état d'âme*, it can only be a small part of what the artist has in him to say'. John, with his sketch-book in his hand, would express his enchantment with the scene before him in terms almost direct. Back in his studio he would take the squared-up studies (why, if he had not intended to use them for another purpose would he have squared them up?) and made of them, usually in oils, less often in watercolour, the bases of subtly, although minimally, different versions of their subjects. Edward Bawden, who often worked with him in the field, described his methods in a letter to me of 24 April 1979.

Quiet Evening
This squared-up pencil sketch of Christine and John's sister Barbara was done in preparation for the wood engraving illustrated on page 63. 11¼" x 9¼", c.1924.
Private Collection

Sketch-book drawings were called for in the summer months & transformed into paintings in the winter. Mysterious operations that then took place in the studio can only be guessed at. Did he, I wonder, carefully enlarge the sketch book drawing by the laborious method of squaring up? How he began the painting having squared it up & re-drawn it I do not know. Once he showed me a drawer full of paintings which had been half begun, with pale washes of colour here & there, unresolved paintings, & I wondered whether he would work on them again or had they been put aside incomplete as a record. An examination of the drawings might reveal a good deal about his method of working. What I feel more sure about is that he panicked not at all, that to extricate a drawing he did not passionately scratch or slash it & probably never rushed off to the bathroom to wash the paper clean. Such behaviour would be out of character. He told me, I remember, that he never experienced a crisis. That admission suggests that a painting might peter out, die gracefully in his arms & John by no means heartbroken would begin by drawing it afresh.

An understanding of the process which took place in the studio is essential to an appreciation of John Nash's work. While some believe that his watercolours constitute his highest achievement, I venture to put the comparison differently: namely that his major works are those carried out, or at least completed, indoors. By a variety of modifications – of the angles of the surface of fields, of hedges, the simplifications of complex subjects such as trees – at his

Marloes Bay, Pembrokeshire
Watercolour, 15″ x 23″, 1961.
It was probably Nash's interest
in the underlying abstract
forms of landscape that
stimulated him to paint views
such as this.
*Private Collection/Photo:
Royal Academy of Arts*

best he seemed even to emphasize their complexity while making them in fact more 'legible'. His penetrating perception of their essential character combined with his rare power of interpreting his perception makes the spectator feel that he is looking with poetic insight at the subject itself. It is possible to exaggerate the distinction between his oils and his watercolours. He made innumerable watercolours outdoors as bases for oils made in his studio, but also many watercolours imbued with the qualities that distinguished his finest oils, though these were almost certainly either begun outdoors, or, like the large majority of his oils, completed in the studio from studies made outdoors.

'In looking at a landscape', he said to me, 'its abstract features appeal pretty quickly. Although representational I am primarily interested in the structure underneath, though I hope not obviously. In fact such changes as I make are based more on selection than specific alteration'. And with regard to subject, 'I am extremely interested in "close-ups", in half a haystack as much as in a wide sweep of landscape'.

There are, and have been, painters who, by a highly personal style, clearly reflect, consciously or not, something of themselves, of their own 'vision' into their work. Of this private vision, however, he appears to have been scarcely aware. 'If I've got a private vision' he said, 'it must be so private that I hardly know it myself'[36].

Suffolk Harvest
Oil on canvas, 24″ x 35″, c.
1935. The consistency of
Nash's depiction of landscape
can be seen by comparing this
view to *Late Summer, Stoke-
by-Nayland* (page 82), painted
in 1951.
*Private Collection/Photo: New
Grafton Gallery*

John Nash was happy with his subjects. And happy with
his subjects in themselves – in so far as a landscape can be
detached from accompanying phenomena – from wind,
rain, fog, dazzling sunlight, the fall of evening – everything
extraneous and liable to affect it, except snow which, until
his later years, was a constant delight. And on these chosen
subjects he concentrated with a serene intensity that gives
his finest paintings and watercolours a place among the
English masterpieces of landscape.

Surely the work of no other serious painter of our time
altered so little as John's; there is no radical difference
between 'The Cornfield' of 1918 and 'Frozen Ponds' of
forty-one years later. Apart from the greater complexity of
'Frozen Ponds', both express the same intense love of his
subject, unaffected to an extraordinary degree by the work
of other painters, a love intensely direct, and imbued by a
reticent nobility. I remember Paul expressing amusement at
how seldom John ever looked at paintings or seemed to
think about them, or read about them and that the sole
inspiration for his landscape was landscape. His vision, at
its most characteristic, was lucid and direct, interrupted by
nothing, not even by everyday – or almost everyday –
natural phenomena. And these qualities characterised his
best work until the end of his life.

In spite of the respect he had always been accorded, John is apt to be judged as somewhat inferior to Paul, and it is easy to see why. Although his outlook remained basically English Paul was thoroughly conversant with the art of the Continent as well as that of the major British painters, which gave his art variety and an aura of sophistication. He spent time in London and Oxford, visited the Continent, and was acquainted with many people capable of enhancing an artist's reputation, and even occasionally praised his own work in the Press under an assumed name. His correspondence with Gordon Bottomley, it is reasonable to suppose, was carried on at such length and detail over so long a period so that it would furnish informative material for a biography, besides his own unfinished autobiography, *Outline*. None of this – except his pseudonymous self-praise, which he regretted deeply, of his own work – is remotely to his discredit, yet as he desired, it brought his work – the subject of wide-ranging literary appreciation – before a large public and earned him the high reputation that he fully deserves.

John was in every respect the contrary. He was to a rare degree uninterested in the work of other artists, except that of his painter friends and his students. As an adult he spent

Wintry Evening, a Pond
Watercolour, 15¼″ x 21¾″, signed and dated 1958. This pond is in the grounds of Great Glenham House near Saxmundham in Suffolk, where Nash often stayed as a guest of the Earl of Cranbrook.
Private Collection

scarcely any time in London at all and when he taught at Oxford he lived in the country, removed from the social life of the town. Apart from some very brief 'Who's Who-ish' notes he wrote nothing autobiographical, though in his vast wartime flow of letters to Christine there is an intimation that he would have liked them preserved. 'Do keep my letters, my love', he once wrote, 'They are the only form of diary I keep and I express most of my thoughts to you if not all'. Apart from John Lewis's highly informative book which, however, concentrates on his work as an illustrator, Frederick Gore's introduction to the catalogue of his Royal Academy exhibition, a booklet by Sydney Schiff, articles in the national and East Anglian newspapers, mostly enthusiastic, especially relating to his Royal Academy exhibition, the professional journals and a chapter in my *Modern English Painters*, relatively little has been written about him. He is indeed much admired when he is known and his pictures regularly bought – occasionally for very high prices – but compared with Paul he has been subject to relative neglect. Paul, in spite of his early recurrent doubts about the wisdom of John's choice of a career, could have been neither a more ardent supporter nor a more devoted brother. Unambitious though he was, towards the end of his life John used at times to feel a little sad at his lack of acclaim.

In spite of his regular seasonal travels during the last three decades or so of his life, John was basically rooted in East Anglia, and his social relations were mainly confined to friendly neighbours. So local a figure did John become that he bears comparison even with Stanley Spencer, known as 'Cookham' at the Slade, whose identification with his native place was even more intimate and of longer duration than John's with Wormingford. But however ardent his feelings for Wormingford they did not prevent him, indeed encouraged him, to enhance his response to his chosen environment, by working in many places from Cornwall to Skye, from the Gower Peninsula to the coast of Norfolk and Suffolk. Indeed paradoxically this artist, so devoted to the region where he had chosen to live, in fact made a wider-ranging panorama of the landscape of Britain than any of his contemporaries. But it was primarily his power of imbuing ordinary landscapes with a poetic aura, to a lesser degree his poetic yet scholarly portrayal of plants and his witty illustrations that place him, at his best, among the memorable artists of his time.

Notes

1. John Nash *The Artist Plantsman*, (Anthony d'Offay 1976).

2. *Outline, an autobiography and other writings*, by Paul Nash, 1949, p. 118.

3. Ibid, p. 59.

4. Ibid, p. 133.

5. Paul Nash, MS.

6. *Poet & Painter*, being the correspondence between Gordon Bottomley and Paul Nash, 1910–46, edited by Claude Colleer Abbot & Anthony Bertram, 1955, p. 67.

7. Ibid.

8. An accomplished but unjustly forgotten artist. He dropped 'Harvey' and was known as Claughton Pellew.

9. *John Nash, the Painter as Illustrator* by John Lewis, 1978, pp. 34–35.

10. *Poet & Painter*, p. 67.

11. *Paint & Prejudice* by C. R. W. Nevinson, 1937, p. 63–64.

12. A loan exhibition of works by Pre-Raphaelite painters from collections in Lancashire, held at the Tate Gallery July-September 1913. 'Again' refers to the Pre-Raphaelite exhibition of works from Birmingham held from December 1911 – March 1912.

13. Lena Dare, who had married the Hon. Maurice Brett, son of Lord Esher, to whom the Roman Camp belonged. Carrington was staying with his daughter, her friend the Hon. Dorothy Brett, a fellow-student at the Slade who was later to join D. H. Lawrence in Mexico.

14. Interview with David Brown and Joseph Darracott, of the Imperial War Museum, about his World War I experiences, on 4 March 1974.

15. 'Artists in an Age of Conflict'. Imperial War Museum, Department of Sound Records. Reel 014 (accession no. 000323/05).

16. *Outline, an autobiography and other writings*, by Paul Nash, pp. 208, 209.

17. *Paul Nash*, by Anthony Bertram, 1955, p. 95.

18. *Poet & Painter*, pp. 98–99.

19. *Artists' Rifles Gazette*, January 1935, p. 5.

20. 'Artists in the Age of Conflict', Reel 01 (accession no. 000323/05).

21. 'Artists in an Age of Conflict', Reel 02 (accession no. 000323/05).

22. Op. cit, p. 101.

23. *The London Mercury*, November 1928.

24. Op. cit, pp. 83–85.

25. Op. cit, p. 94.

26. *Poet & Painter*.

27. Op. cit, p. 19.

28. *John Nash* by John Lewis, p. 95.

29. *Poet & Painter*, p. 266.

30. A booklet published by Anthony d'Offay, 1976, to accompany an exhibition at his gallery of John Nash's wood engravings, illustrations and drawings of plants.

31. 'Flower Drawing' by Jennifer Andrews, *Leisure Painter*, November 1979.

32. Op. cit, p. 28.

33. Op. cit, p. 28.

34. 'Idealism', *The Art News*, 12 May 1910.

35. Article, originally published in *The New Age*, which appeared in the catalogue of an Exhibition of Paintings by Harold Gilman and Charles Ginner, at the Goupil Gallery, 18 April to 9 May 1914.

36. *John Nash, A Painter in the Country*. BBC Television, directed and produced by John Read, with a commentary by Ronald Blythe, 1962.

Chronology

1893   11 April – John Northcote Nash born in London.

1901   Nash family moved to Wood Lane House, Iver Heath, Buckinghamshire.

1905–09   at Langley House preparatory school.

1910–12   Educated at Wellington College.

1910   4 February – Caroline Nash died.

1912   Worked as junior reporter for *Middlesex & Buckinghamshire Advertiser*.
Encouraged by brother Paul in his watercolours and comic drawings.
Watercolour accepted by New English Art Club.
Walking trip in East Anglia with Claughton Pellew.

1913   Joint exhibition with Paul at Dorien Leigh Gallery, South Kensington, London.
First acquaintance with Dora Carrington.
Member of Friday Club.
16 December – Brighton Public Art Gallery – participated in interim show of 'The Camden Town Group, Vorticists & Others' leading to formation of:

1914   The London Group – first exhibition, 5 March at the Goupil Gallery, London.
October – sworn in as a Special Constable.

1915   Closely associated with the Cumberland Market Group – Bevan, Gilman and Ginner.
April – exhibited with them at Goupil Gallery, London.

1916   September – enlisted in Artists' Rifles.

1916–18   On active service in France.

1918   Spring – commissioned as Official War Artist.
May – married to Christine Kühlenthal.
June – shared studio with Paul at Chalfont St Peter.
Painted 'Oppy Wood', 'Over the Top'; 'The Cornfield', first peacetime picture, bought by Sir Edward Marsh.

1919   Illustrations for *Dressing Gowns & Glue*.
Became Art Critic for the *London Mercury*.

1919–21   Lived at Gerrard's Cross with summer excursions to the Chilterns and Gloucestershire.

1920   Member of newly-founded Society of Wood Engravers.

1921   First one-man show at the Goupil Gallery, London.
Moved to Lane End House, Meadle, near Princes Risborough.
Increasing interest in plants, growing and painting them.

1922   First visits to East Anglia.

1924–29   Taught at Ruskin School of Art, Oxford.

1925   Swift's *Directions to Servants* published.
Visits to Bath and Bristol.

1927   *Poisonous Plants* published.

1929   Rented summer cottage at Wormingford.

1930   Exhibition at Goupil Gallery.
Birth of son, William.

1933   *The Curious Gardener* by Jason Hill published.

1934–40   Teaching in the Design School at the Royal College of Art.

1935   *Flowers and Faces* by H. E. Bates published.
Death of son, William.

1937   Executed large design for Paris Exhibition.
Visit to Bristol with Eric Ravilious.

1939   First visit to Gower Peninsula, Glamorgan, Wales with Christine.
Joined Royal Observer Corps.

1940   Appointed Official War Artist to the Admiralty, serving in Plymouth, Swansea and Bristol.
Elected Associate of Royal Academy.
Applied for transfer to active service.

1941   March – commissioned as Captain, later Acting Major, in Royal Marines, on staff of C. in C. in Rosyth and Portsmouth.

1945   Moved to Bottengoms farmhouse, near Wormingford.
Re-joined staff at RCA.

1946   Death of Paul Nash.

1951   Elected RA.
The Natural History of Selborne published.

1954   Retrospective exhibition at Leicester Galleries, London.

1956   Visit to Ironbridge with Edward Bawden and Carel Weight.

1957   First of regular trips to Isle of Skye.

1958	Began teaching annual plant illustration courses at Flatford Mill Field Centre.		Nash CBE RA' at Royal Academy. Awarded an honorary degree by the University of Sussex.
1959	*Happy New Lear* published.	1968	Golden Wedding Anniversary.
1962	First of many painting trips to Cornwall.	1976	Exhibition at Anthony d'Offay's gallery – 'The Artist Plantsman'. Death of Christine Nash.
1964	Awarded CBE.		
1967	Major retrospective exhibition 'John	1977	23 September – death of John Nash.

Principal Exhibitions of work by John Nash

1913	Dorien Leigh Gallery, London – with Paul Nash. 16 December 1913 – 19 January 1914: Brighton Public Art Gallery – 'The Camden Town Group, Vorticists & Others'.	1953	Aldeburgh Festival, Suffolk. Graves Art Gallery, Sheffield.
		1954	Leicester Galleries, London – retrospective.
		1960	Leicester Galleries, London.
1915	Goupil Gallery, London – with the Cumberland Market Group (Robert Bevan, Harold Gilman, and Charles Ginner).	1967	Royal Academy of Arts, London – 'John Nash CBE RA'. The Minories, Colchester
1921	Goupil Gallery, London – first one-man show.	1970	Hamet Gallery, London.
		1971	Worthing Art Gallery.
1930	Goupil Gallery, London.	1973	Anthony d'Offay, London.
1933	The French Gallery, London.	1974	Maltzahn Gallery, London.
1938	Little Burlington Gallery, London.	1976	Anthony d'Offay – 'The Artist Plantsman'.
1939	Goupil Gallery, London.	1978	Blond Fine Art, London – 'Paul Nash and John Nash'.
1950	Harris Museum & Art Gallery, Preston.	1980	Aldeburgh Festival, Suffolk.

Bibliography

The most comprehensive bibliography of the books, booklets, and other graphic work illustrated by John Nash is to be found in John Lewis's excellent book *John Nash the painter as illustrator* with a Foreword by Wilfrid Blunt (The Pendomer Press, 1978).

The following is a selective list of books, catalogues, and other writings with reference to John Nash's life and work:

Alphabet and Image No. 3, December 1946 'The Engravings & Book Decorations of John Nash' Frances Sarzano.
The Artist Plantsman John Nash (Anthony d'Offay, 1976).
Artists at Curwen Pat Gilmour (Tate Gallery, 1977).
British Wood Engraving of the 20th Century a personal view Albert Garrett (Scolar, 1980).
Country Life 7 September 1967 'John Nash's Home-Grown Vision' Christopher Neve.
The History of Wood Engraving Douglas Percy Bliss (Dent, 1928).

Modern English Painters 2: Lewis to Moore Sir John Rothenstein (Eyre & Spottiswoode, 1956).
John Nash CBE RA Catalogue for an exhibition of paintings and drawings by John Nash with an introduction by Frederick Gore ARA (Royal Academy of Arts, 1967).
Paul Nash Anthony Bertram (Faber, 1955).
Outline: an autobiography and other writings Paul Nash (Faber, 1949).
Paint & Prejudice C. R. W. Nevinson (Methuen, 1937).
Picture Post 1 April 1939 'John Nash' Dr John Rothenstein (Great British Masters Series No. 27).
Poet and Painter, being the Correspondence between Gordon Bottomley and Paul Nash 1910–1946 (Oxford, 1955).
The Sunday Times Colour Supplement 31 August 1975 'A Sense of Place' William Feaver.
The Woodcut Vol. 3 1929 'The Wood Engravings of John Nash' W. A. Thorpe.

Index